Amish Brides
of Willow Creek

Book One: Sibling Rivalry

Samantha Jillian Bayarr

❧Sibling Rivalry❧

CHAPTER 1

"Is he dead?"

Levinia Miller set her gaze in the direction of Willow Creek where her sister pointed to the *Englischer* who lay face-down on the muddy embankment. The gentle current of the creek washed over his feet as they hung over the edge, forcing them to sway. If not for the length of his body anchored safely ashore, he'd have likely drifted down to the next county. The very possibility of the man lying there dead made Levinia tremble with an unnatural fear. A fear that only comes from witnessing death first-hand.

She stiffened her upper lip and narrowed her brow with defiance. "There's only one way to find out!"

Bethany shook her head furiously. "You won't get me to go over there to look. I ain't touching a dead body."

Levinia knew all too well the feel of a dead body as the life drained from it, but she pushed back the memory.

"No one said anything about touching him, you chicken! If he's dead, we'll run back to the barn and call the law. They can come take care of him."

If their father was here, he'd most likely tell his daughters to stay back and let the law handle it, but Levinia felt a sort of morbid curiosity that had suddenly taken charge of her.

She *had* to know if the man was dead.

Levinia swallowed back fear as she grabbed hold of the willow branches that hung over the embankment, using them to leverage herself to avoid slipping in the mud. Recent rains had raised the level of the creek enough to soak the grassy area along the bank to where each step she took caused her to sink. Rich, black soil stuck to the bottoms of her black, lace-up shoes and splattered the hem of her dress. Laboriously lifting each foot against the slight suction of the mud made for a long walk of the short distance between her and the *Englischer.*

"Wait!" Bethany called.

Levinia stopped abruptly, whipped her head back toward her sister, heart pounding. "Don't scare me like that. You made me think there was a snake or something coming after me!"

Bethany rolled her eyes. "What if he's dangerous?"

Looking back at the *Englischer,* who was now only a few feet from her—still face-down in the mud, Levinia shook her head. "How dangerous can he be like that?

"He could be faking! What if he's faking?"

Levinia stared at the lifeless man. "Why would he be faking?"

"So he can attack or *kill* whoever finds him!"

"That's *narrish*. If he wanted to do that, he would probably hide behind a tree instead of pushing his face in the mud, wouldn't you think? He looks hurt. And who knows how long he's been lying there. He could be dead!"

Bethany rolled her eyes again. "I doubt it. We'd probably be able to smell him by now. Besides, I don't see any buzzards pecking at him!"

"That's horrible!"

"Maybe. But it's the truth!"

Levinia sighed impatiently and continued on the muddy path toward the stranger. The gurgle of the rushing creek muffled most of the sound this close to the water, and Levinia wondered if anyone would be able to hear her if she should need to scream for help. The closer she came to the man, the faster her heart hammered against her ribs. With her sister's words rattling her confidence and her past history with death so close to her, she approached him warily.

The late afternoon sun warmed her back, sending a bead of sweat trickling down the bodice of her dress. If not for the breeze drifting from the chilly creek, she'd probably faint from the late October heat. Swiping at her dampened brow, she bent over the man to check if he was breathing. As far as she could tell, he wasn't moving. The bird's song in the willow trees overhead and the flow of creek water rushing by intruded upon her ability to hear him breathe. Since he was face-down, she was unable to detect the rise and fall of his chest. On impulse, Levinia nudged at his heel with the toe of her shoe.

He rolled over and sputtered, barely breathing—but breathing nonetheless.

Startled by his alarming reaction, Levinia jumped backward, ready to run if he posed a threat.

Groaning, the man looked helpless and in a lot of pain, though he didn't open his eyes.

"Looks like he ain't dead!" Bethany hollered from the safety of the willow tree.

Thank the Lord, Levinia thought, as she blew out a sigh of relief.

Kneeling down beside the stranger, Levinia leaned back on her haunches and pulled the man's head into her lap. Using her apron to wipe the mud from his face, she felt warmth radiating from him like a surge of static electricity. The hot sun had surely warmed him, but there was more to it than that. With compassion, Levinia gently caressed his temples, smoothing back his dampened, mud-streaked curls. Running her hand along his strong jawline, the stubble that peppered his smooth, sun-kissed face prickled the tips of her fingers.

Though he looked to be a little worn and dirty, she couldn't help but notice how handsome he was.

Her subconscious allowed the steady flow of the creek to occupy her thoughts as she breathed out the simplest of prayers.

Please Lord, let him be alright.

"What are you doing, Levinia?" Bethany called from behind the willow tree, where she'd been hiding her face.

Ignoring her sister, Levinia continued to stroke the man's face, allowing her fingers to make a trail through his auburn curls and willing him to open his eyes. His breathing, though a little labored, was steady.

He groaned again, his eyes fluttering.

"Are you in pain?"

No answer.

"Can you tell me your name?"

Still, no answer.

Whoever he was, he certainly did not look Amish, though Levinia couldn't think of a single reason he'd be walking along the bank of the creek dressed the way he was. His muddy shirt, a blue button-up, most likely his Sunday attire, hugged strong arms and a muscular chest. It was still slightly tucked into the narrow waist of his black dress-pants. Beside him, curiously, lay a black hat that resembled an Amish hat—perhaps from another community. Not far from him, she noticed a backpack wedged in the reeds closer to the creek.

He clutched his left side as he let out another deep groan. Slowly moving her hand over his, Levinia palpitated his ribs lightly, noting him wince from the pain. Unbuttoning the middle buttons of his shirt, she slipped her hand into the opening, glancing at the bruises and swelling over the area where he couldn't tolerate her touch. Though they didn't feel broken, his ribs were most likely cracked, and that could be just as serious. She would never be able to move him unless she bound his ribs, or she might risk breaking them. Unpinning her apron, Levinia wrapped it around his torso and knotted the ends at his right side.

"You shouldn't be touching him," Bethany called from the safe distance of the willow tree. "Do you want me to get *Daed?*"

Levinia shook her head, not wanting to take her eyes off the man—this beautiful man that she hoped would wake up.

She cradled his head once more and his lashes fluttered as he suddenly looked up at her with chocolate-brown eyes.

Reaching up with muddy fingers, he covered her hand that cupped his jaw and sent her a pleading look.

"Can you tell me your name?" she asked.

"N—Nate."

"I'm Levinia and I'm going to help you."

He smiled weakly and closed his fingers over hers just before his eyes closed again.

Panic ran through her veins like icy creek water.

"Don't leave me," Nate whispered.

I wouldn't dream of it, Levinia thought.

Turning toward her sister, Levinia hollered impatiently. "Come over here and help me get him up."

Her voice seemed to startle Nate. He turned his head toward her, allowing her to feel the knot on the side of his head. Thankfully, he didn't seem to be bleeding from anywhere that she could see. She suspected he'd traveled some distance, and had likely walked down to the creek to get a drink because he didn't seem dehydrated, and she hoped it would help him recover.

"I already told you I ain't coming over there. I'm going back to the barn to call for an ambulance."

"*Nee,*" Levinia begged. "Please help me get him up."

She had already been down that road and she would not let history repeat itself.

Bethany began to trudge through the mud toward them, muttering complaints under her breath. Levinia tuned her out, putting her full attention on the handsome stranger. She wouldn't let her sister call for an ambulance. She would do everything she could to prevent it, even if it meant threatening to tell their *daed* some of the secrets Bethany had recently confided in her.

Calling for an ambulance hadn't helped Daniel.

She'd watched helplessly while her twin had bled to death waiting for that ambulance, when the community doctor could have gotten to him faster. Levinia had panicked at the sight of all the blood and had made the call from the barn when Daniel had caught his wrist on the barbed-wire fence.

The pain and guilt she carried with her from that day haunted her even now that two years had passed.

Daed would certainly make the same call for an *Englischer*.

No, there would be no ambulance for *this* man.

As long as Nate was breathing, Levinia would devote herself to caring for him and nursing him back to health.

CHAPTER 2

"Why can't *you* take his cold, wet feet?"

"Stop complaining, Bethany, and just help me—please!"

Levinia looped the insides of her elbows in Nate's armpits and hefted him up until his head rested against her ribcage. Assessing him to be around six feet tall, she wasn't surprised at the weight of his muscular frame. It wouldn't be easy toting the dead-weight of a semi-conscious man the distance to their farm, but Levinia was as stubborn as could be. She'd managed to talk her sister into putting him up in the loft above their barn, safe from their father's strict supervision.

Since Daniel's death, their *daed* had mostly kept to himself, but he constantly reminded them of the rules of his *haus*. Levinia knew it was because he feared harm would come to them if they were out of his immediate sight for too long, but she also knew that with a farm to tend to, he couldn't watch them every minute and didn't have the time to enforce the rules the way he would prefer.

Bethany stumbled and dropped Nate's feet. He let out a deep groan and pulled his hand toward his ribs as Levinia stopped abruptly to prevent his head from slipping away from her.

"You need to be more careful carrying him," Levinia reprimanded. "If his ribs are broken they could pierce one of his organs and he would bleed to death."

"It ain't my fault he's so heavy! You act like I meant to drop him."

Levinia narrowed her gaze on Bethany, but held her tongue to keep from letting on just how irritated she was with the girl. She knew she couldn't move Nate without her sister's help, which put her in an unfortunate state of dependence on her. Bethany would be certain to find a way to use this *favor* to her advantage as it suited her. Bethany was a selfish girl, but lucky for her, Levinia loved her in spite of it.

For this reason, Levinia patiently waited for Bethany to resume hold of Nate's feet so they could continue on to their barn. Until then, Levinia let her mind drift to memories of her last moments with Daniel. She bent down and rested her chin on Nate's head, swallowing back tears. Was she doing the right thing? What if she couldn't save him? Would his death be her fault too? Surely *Daed* would blame her the same way he blamed her for Daniel's death. She would never forget the look in her father's eyes that day.

He hadn't looked at her since.

Bethany hoisted Nate's feet onto her sides and pushed out a disparaging breath. "I'm ready. Let's go before I drop him again!"

Levinia gladly broke from her reverie. She had spent the past two years trying not to think of Daniel, but her twin was suddenly plaguing her thoughts. She convinced herself that each stride they conquered was one step closer to saving Nate. If they could just get him comfortable in the loft, he would heal from the wounds that encumbered him. Saving Nate wouldn't bring back Daniel, but it would serve as penance for her foolish decisions that day that her father claimed had contributed to Daniel's demise. Decisions she vowed never to repeat.

A few more steps put them behind the barn. "Go see where *Daed* is. He needs to be *gut* and busy at whatever he's doing so we have enough time to get Nate up the stairs."

"How do you know his name?" Bethany demanded through gritted teeth.

"He told me."

"When did he tell you? He's knocked out."

"He told me before you came over to help me move him. What does it matter? Just go see where *Daed* is—please!"

Bethany cast her sister an angry look before leaving to do her bidding.

Alone once again with Nate, Levinia sank to the grass and rested his head in her lap. She pushed back his curls behind his ears wondering what it would be like to have such a handsome man for a husband. Levinia knew better than to hope for such a thing. Not only was she responsible for Bethany and her father and their farm, she was as Plain as a woman could be—especially compared to her sister, who had never had any trouble gaining the attention from the boys in the community.

Please, Lord, bless me with a man such as this to love me, Levinia whispered.

She felt foolish even asking for such a prideful prayer, but she meant it with all her heart.

Bethany came back around the back side of the barn. "*Daed's* under the big oak tree in the yard taking a nap."

Levinia noted the direction of the barn's shadow. "Is it that late already? We need to hurry before he gets up and wants his supper and I don't have it ready for him before evening chores."

"I agree," Bethany said. "Let's get him upstairs to the loft. I'll stay with him while you make the evening meal so *Daed* won't get suspicious."

Levinia felt a twinge of jealousy toward her sister, who had no idea what real responsibility was. Being nearly five years her senior, Levinia had been taking care of Bethany since she was four years old—since *Mamm's* death. But now the girl was almost eighteen and she was still too dependent on Levinia.

Truth be told, Levinia had only herself to blame. She'd catered to her sister and had not enforced the teachings that an Amish woman should know to do by this age. For Levinia, it had always been easier to do the work herself than to struggle with getting her sister to do her fair share.

Though she'd taken on the role of *mamm* to Bethany, she wasn't her *mamm,* and could not get her to do much without an argument. Rather than having *Daed* discipline her by taking the strap to her back-side, Levinia had allowed her sister to rebel too often to help her to be responsible this late in her life. Now it would be up to Bethany to mature enough to understand the importance of learning the skills needed to be a married woman. Levinia knew Bethany was nowhere near being ready for such an important role; she was too busy enjoying the attention of every young man in the community to settle for just one. It angered Levinia that Bethany couldn't even be responsible for herself, and suddenly, she wanted to take responsibility for Nate!

"Perhaps *you* should make *Daed* his evening meal for a change. I do all the work around here while you flit around making whimsical play of your life instead of being responsible!"

Bethany scowled. "I do plenty of chores around here!"

"Not without an argument."

Bethany dropped Nate's feet causing him to clutch his side and groan. "If you think I do nothing around here, then you can take him upstairs yourself while I go tell *Daed* you're hiding an *Englischer* in the loft. You aren't too old for *Daed* to take you out behind the barn for a *gut,* sound lashing like our cousin's get from their *Daed.* "

Levinia was fuming, but dared not show her anger to her sister. She needed her help *and* her loyalty at this moment. For reasons unknown even to herself, she wasn't willing to let Nate depart from her life without a fight. She supposed it stemmed from the losses she'd suffered—especially with her twin's recent death. Whatever the reason, she felt that *Gott,* Himself had a hand in it somehow.

For that reason alone, she would have to tread water with her sister's immature temperament, and succumb to the girl's whims. It filled her with a deep resentment toward her sister, but she pushed it down, just as she'd been doing most of her life. Because of Bethany, she had not been allowed to enjoy her youth enough to appreciate it. She'd been a mother and caretaker of her sister and her father since she was a mere child herself, and her *mamm's* death had in a way cheated her out of a life as well.

Levinia sighed impatiently. "Please help me get him upstairs and stop using threats to get your own way. Since you've helped me get him this far, *Daed* will know I didn't get him here by myself, so we will *both* get a sound lashing. You can either work *with* me and we can get him upstairs before *Daed* wakes up and sees him, or we can stand here and argue a little longer and get into trouble. It's your choice little *schweschder*."

Bethany narrowed her gaze on Levinia. "I'll help you get him up there, but not for *you*. I'll do it for Nate. After all, he's pretty handsome."

Levinia held her tongue even though she would enjoy giving her sister a sound lashing herself.

CHAPTER 3

Levinia rushed through the cooking, knowing that every minute she spent preparing her *daed's* evening meal meant another minute Bethany was spending alone with Nate. She'd wanted to be there in case he woke up—in case he asked for her.

Jealousy rose up in her again at the thought of Nate making a connection with Bethany if he should wake, especially since she felt she'd already made one with him. She felt foolish for not wanting Nate to like her sister, but she'd never had the chance to be so close to a man before, and Bethany had been on so many dates, she'd made her way around the young men in the community more than once. Levinia, on the other hand, had never had even one date. She'd been too busy being the responsible one while Bethany sneaked out of the *haus* so many times it ceased to bother her anymore.

Her father came in before she was able to set everything on the table and grumbled without looking at his daughter. "Supper's late."

"I'm sorry *Daed.* I must have gotten behind in my chores."

He took the plate she offered without looking up. "Where is your *schweschder?*"

"She's probably picking apples and lost track of time. I'll fetch her right away."

Her father tasted the stew without praying first, his long, wiry beard dipping in the bowl as he lowered his head to take another bite.

Levinia escaped through the kitchen door before he could say another word. If he found out she'd lied to him, he'd surely take the switch to her back-side. She ran to the barn and up the outside staircase to the loft apartment that had always been intended for Daniel to use during the first year of his marriage, but sadly, he'd never gotten the chance. It pricked her heart to think of the things her *bruder* would never be able to do, such as marry and have *kinner*. It filled her with guilt. She supposed it was one of the reasons she didn't date. There was a part of her that thought she didn't deserve to be happy since Daniel wasn't able to do those things either.

Levinia pushed down the guilt over Daniel's death and quickly made her way up the stairs to the loft. Entering the small bedroom, Levinia covered her mouth to prevent the gasp from escaping her lips. She watched in shock as Bethany bent over Nate, whose bare chest lay exposed. From what she could tell, the girl had torn a bed-sheet into long bandage strips and used them to bind his ribs. She had just finished tying the last strip when she noticed her sister staring blankly at her.

She smiled proudly.

"He woke up for a minute, but he passed out when I moved him to wrap his ribs."

Levinia rushed to Nate's side, leaning close to check his breathing. "You should have waited for me to come back. You could have seriously hurt him by moving him yourself!"

Bethany waved a casual hand at her older sister.

"Why are you yelling at me? I got him all fixed up."

"Did you check his ribs to be certain they were set before you wrapped him?"

Bethany shook her head. "I don't know what you mean."

"Exactly!" Levinia scolded her. "Now I'm going to have to cause this poor *mann* more pain by undoing the bandages to be certain his ribs are in the correct place, and then rewrap him."

"I'm sorry. I was only trying to help."

"*Daed* wants you at the supper table," Levinia said through gritted teeth.

"But…"

"Just go! I need to fix this the same way I take care of everything for you."

Bethany fisted her hips angrily. "What is *that* supposed to mean?

Levinia took a step toward her sister. "It means you need to grow up and start thinking of someone other than yourself. You are almost eighteen years old and you don't even know how to cook or do laundry or…"

"I help you with all those things!"

"Hanging up one dress and then running off does not earn you the skills needed to be on your own. What would you do if I wasn't here to do everything for you?"

Bethany shook her head knowingly. "That's not going to happen. Where would you have to go, *schweschder?* We *both* know you will most likely end up a spinster."

The comment prickled down Levinia's spine like the sharp quills on a porcupine.

"And so shall you be," Levinia retorted. "Unless you learn the skills you need to keep a husband."

Bethany cocked her head sideways and smiled.

"I *know* what keeps a husband happy!"

Levinia let a gasp escape her lips at her sister's brazen words. "You should confess that evil from your mind at once! If the Bishop—or *Daed* heard you speak of such things you'd be shunned for sure and for certain."

"Maybe if you'd take down that wall you've built around yourself and go on a date for once in your life, you might just know what I'm talking about."

Levinia's eyes widened. "You've done *that* on a date?"

Looking over at Nate, Bethany shushed her sister. "Of course not! I'm talking about kissing!"

Sadly, Levinia had never been kissed, and didn't hold out much hope for such a thing. Her thoughts turned to Nate and wondered if the kiss she'd placed on his forehead counted. She supposed only if he'd kissed her back would it have counted. The very thought of it sent a warmth through her veins that surged toward her toes.

She let her gaze wander back toward Nate, who lay sleeping on the bed, oblivious to their rather brazen conversation. It was inappropriate to speak of such things in private, let alone to be speaking of them within earshot of a man. Some women in the community would talk of those things during quilting bees or work-bees, but Levinia had only ever listened. This was the first time she'd participated in such bold talk.

Levinia narrowed her gaze at her sister. "I imagine you've kissed every single *mann* in this community."

Bethany smiled. "You've imagined correctly."

"That's shameful!"

"What is shameful, dear *schweschder,* is that *you* haven't kissed even one of them!"

Levinia couldn't deny the pitiful truth in her sister's statement any more than she could deny her yearning for such an experience. Looking over at Nate once more, she swallowed down the lump that choked her, knowing that such a man as handsome as he would *never* find her attractive enough to kiss.

Nate's hand reached for hers, startling her out of her reverie.

"Water," he said, his dry lips parting slightly.

Though his eyes remained closed, Levinia was happy he'd reached for her rather than for her sister. The glare Bethany shot her let her know her sister didn't feel the same as she did.

Levinia poured water into a glass from the pitcher at his bedside and scooped her hand under his head to assist him. She placed the glass to his lips and tipped it just enough to allot him small sips. He looked up at her with weary eyes. Levinia couldn't help but notice the pain in their chocolaty depths.

"I need to check the bandages around your ribs," she said cautiously. "It might hurt a little, but I think *mei schweschder* may have forgotten to set your ribs before she bound them."

He nodded his consent and Levinia set to work undoing the damage her sister had done to this poor man.

The screen door to the loft slammed behind her and she knew Bethany had left in a huff. She didn't care. She was glad to be rid of her. Bethany had always been selfish and immature, and this situation was proving to be no exception. She pushed back her disappointment in her sister and concentrated on tending to Nate's injuries.

Wincing, Nate let her know every time she put too much pressure on his sore ribs. She hated hurting him, and repeatedly apologized, but didn't feel it was enough for the torture she was certain she was putting him through. Thankfully, none were broken clean through, but she could feel two spots that were cracked. Pressing them tightly into place before binding them, Nate let out a low groan, noting his discomfort.

"I'm only doing what's necessary to assure proper healing of these ribs," she quickly said in her defense.

"I know you're doing the right thing," he said gently. "But sometimes doing the right thing can be...downright painful."

His accent sounded familiar, but his choice of wording seemed "put-on", she thought. She wondered if he could indeed be Amish, but his clothing and speech would suggest he was either an *Englischer,* or *posing* as one.

CHAPTER 4

Nate looked up at Levinia as she finished binding his ribs. He felt guilty for deceiving her, but he also knew keeping his privacy was necessary in order to conclude the soul-searching endeavor he'd set himself on. He wanted more than anything to let her know he was Amish, to confide in her how much he battled the decision to get baptized, but he feared she might be inclined to persuade his decision in one direction or the other. And he hadn't yet decided for himself.

Even though his cousin, Adam, expected him to bring in the harvest, he wasn't ready to leave this

Angel of Mercy just yet. Her gentle, loving care made him crave more of the same. Surely such a lovely creature as she had a beau, but he could hope she didn't—couldn't he? He focused his gaze on the dark blonde tendril that waved across her smooth, pink cheek as she leaned over him tightening the strips of cotton cloth over his ribs. Her deep green eyes were filled with caring, but seemed lonely. Could it be she didn't have a beau after all? He knew it was selfish and foolish to hope for such a thing—especially since he barely knew her, but he couldn't help himself.

"If you're hungry, I made some lamb stew."

He quickly nodded. Lamb stew was one of his favorites.

She knew she would have to wait until her father went about his evening chores before she could bring Nate anything to eat, but she hoped to impress him with one of her best supper dishes. She knew it was foolish to think such things, but she'd heard many of the women in the community talk of *gut* food being the *way* to a *mann's* heart, and she aimed to find out if that was true.

As she finished tying the last of the cotton strips across his ribs, she tugged at the quilt at the end of the bed, wishing she didn't have to cover up his bare, muscular torso. But she had to accept that keeping him warm would help him heal and keep infection at bay.

Nate took note of Levinia's rosy cheeks as her gaze trailed up his chest and settled on his arms and shoulders while she slowly tucked him into the quilt. He was tempted to flex his muscles to impress her, but he resisted, knowing it might embarrass her. Instead, he watched her study him as if she was storing away in her memory the sight of him without his shirt on, and he welcomed her to look as much as she wanted. When her gaze lifted and their eyes met, he remembered her kissing him, and couldn't help but wish he could kiss her back. He'd never felt that before, though he'd been on his fair share of dates.

Most of the young women in his community were only concerned with having a husband, and were not concerned with falling in love. He, on the other hand, intended only to marry for love. His parents had married for love, and they were the happiest pair he knew. Too many folks in his community had troubled marriages and were estranged from each other due to their lack of compatibility—or even love for one another. Many of his friends who had married at a young age just for the sake of marrying were already miserable, and would have to endure a lifetime with the mate they'd chosen for *physical* reasons of desire rather than from true love. If asked, they would deem *him* to be the foolish one, but he knew what he wanted, and that was a mutual love that could endure the test of a lifetime.

"So where did you travel from, if I may be so bold as to ask."

"From a farm in Ohio," was all he dared say.

"So then you know how to plant and harvest?"

"I've lived on a farm all my life," he admitted.

She set a curious gaze on him. "Where were you headed?"

"To work on a farm in this area."

"So you've already found work, then?"

"In a manner of speaking." He looked her straight in the eyes, wondering if she intended to question him until she managed to get it out of him who he was and what he was up to.

"And the ribs…no one *hurt* you, did they?"

Nate shook his head. "I was on the railroad bridge and the train was headed toward me too fast, so I had to jump. I'll take a few cracked ribs over being flattened by a train any day!"

"Does your *familye* live in Ohio?"

He nodded.

"You ask a lot of questions."

She giggled, sending his heart aflutter.

"*Mei daed* always said I was a curious child."

His look softened. "You are anything but a child now."

Her cheeks heated. Was he *flirting* with her? She dared not hope for such a thing, but she almost couldn't help herself. Perhaps he was only flattering her since he was at her mercy and depended on her to take care of him until he regained his strength and his ribs healed some. Was he worried about the care she would give him? Perhaps he felt as if she'd brought him here against his will, which, in a way, she had. He was in a strange place with people he didn't know, and had no idea if she meant him any harm. She felt sorry for him and felt the need to offer him an *out*.

"We have a telephone in the lower part of the barn if you'd like me to call someone for you—so they know you are alright—and where you are."

He smiled. "That won't be necessary. I should be well enough to travel in a few days or so, and I can be on my way then if you want me to."

She didn't want him to leave. If she had her way, he'd stay and help work *her* farm. Perhaps he could even help to bridge the gap between her and her father and restore the closeness they shared before Daniel's death. It saddened her to think of Nate leaving already when he'd only just gotten here. "Those ribs could take a while before they heal—depending on how badly they're cracked."

He couldn't help but smile. It seemed she was as eager for him to stay as he was to be here with her. She was a true angel, and the most beautiful of women he'd ever encountered. "You're probably right. In the meantime, I think I will enjoy having you care for me. But please, don't let your sister do any more doctoring on me."

They both laughed, and he clutched his ribs, holding them until he stopped laughing.

"She means well," Levinia defended her sister, even though she knew better.

She didn't want Nate to think they were careless or would hurt him. She would have to keep a closer eye on her sister when she tended to him in her absence. But perhaps, she would have to engage Bethany in a few more chores to afford her a bigger window of time to care for Nate herself. It would be tricky to maneuver around her *daed's* regular schedule. It was possible that she could give the excuse that she was only trying to give the girl more responsibility to teach her what she needed in order to find a husband. After all, the girl was almost of marrying age, and perhaps her father would appreciate her help in preparing Bethany for her future.

Nate patted her hand, sending a surge of warmth through her. "I'm sure you're right, but I prefer your gentle touch to her rough treatment."

Levinia smiled shyly. She knew he was only complimenting her first-aid skills, but she didn't care.

A compliment was a compliment.

A warm evening breeze scented the loft with freshly mowed hay, and the cricket's song added to the romance that thickened the air between them. Levinia wished she could hold onto this moment as long as she could, knowing she may never have another one like it as long as she lived. If it were up to her, Nate would fall in love with her, and bring happiness to her life again. Though nothing could fill the voids of her lost mother and twin brother, having a husband would help to heal the hurts that kept her sad. She already felt this man's kindness. She didn't need to know who he was to feel that *Gott* had brought him into her life for a reason. And she aimed to find out just what that reason was—if she could keep her father and sister from messing it up for her.

Levinia cleared her throat. "I can get you that stew now if you're ready."

Nate's mouth began to water at the thought of it.

"I was born ready!"

"I won't be but a minute. I hope you like lamb stew and buttermilk biscuits."

"They are my favorite!"

Levinia was pleased to hear that it was his favorite. It was hers too!

Giggling like a young girl, Levinia left him, excitement filling her at the thought of feeding him her best cooking. She would serve him and dote on him as a *fraa* would, hoping he would give her the consideration she desired from him—even if he *was* an *Englischer.*

CHAPTER 5

"What are you doing, *dochder?*"

The deep rumble of her father's voice startled Levinia so profoundly, she dropped the bowl of stew she'd dished up for Nate. The contents splattered onto the wood floor of the kitchen, while the large, ceramic bowl seemed to shatter into an endless splay of pieces.

Though the hot stew burned her ankles where it splattered onto her bare skin, she didn't dare complain in front of her father. Instead, she scrambled to pick up the pieces of broken pottery and then mopped up the stew with a dishrag. All the while, she ignored her father's question, hoping the distraction of the mess would allow her enough time to think of a reasonable answer.

Feigning distraction would not buy her much time, especially since she could see him tapping his boot impatiently on the wood floor. It was something he'd done to show his irritation since she was a child, and she knew her time against his patience was limited. Soon, she would have to give an answer whether she was ready for it not, and whether he was ready to accept it or not. Lately, he was not accepting of whatever she had to say, and so she didn't think it would matter what she said— as long as she said *something.* Any answer was usually better than saying nothing.

She had tried avoiding answering only one time in her life, and it was not a lesson she would risk learning the hard way a second time. Even a lie at this point would be better received than ignoring him. If there was one thing her father did not permit from his *kinner,* it would have to be ignoring him.

"Why are you serving up supper this late? You should be washing the dishes and turning in after you finish. Why didn't you take your meal with Bethany earlier?"

"I was too overheated from the day's chores to eat earlier, so I thought I would have a little of the stew now before tucking away the rest for your afternoon meal tomorrow."

Her voice cracked several times as she spouted off the lie to her father, and she hoped he was too tired to notice. It was her *tell* whenever she wasn't being completely honest, and she'd been that way since she was a child. Instead of calling her on it, he merely grunted and turned toward the stairs. The sun had retired more than an hour ago, and he would retire now too so as to be well-rested to start his day early. He'd kept the same predictable schedule for as long as she could remember. He was a creature of habit, and she was grateful that he would stick to his routine now and leave her alone.

Truth be told, she had grown tired of his prying and disapproval of her every move in recent years—ever since Daniel's death. Her twin's parting from this world had changed her world in too many ways that caused her to despise her present life. There were even times when she'd thought her *daed* would have preferred if *Gott* would have chosen to take *her* instead.

It saddened her to think of her life with such disregard, but her *daed* had all but shunned her since that day. Her father blamed her for Daniel's death. He'd said as much after the funeral when he'd told her he would never again be able to look upon her face as long as she lived. It had made her feel as though they should have put her in the ground right alongside her *bruder* because she'd become dead to her own father from that moment on.

Standing at the bottom of the stairwell, Levinia listened for her father's bedroom door to close before she dared to dish up another bowl of stew for Nate. As soon as he'd finished in the bathroom and was seemingly tucked into bed, Levinia felt she could finally breathe easy. She didn't know why she'd become so afraid of her father in recent years, but she supposed it had stemmed from him taking out his anger over Daniel's death onto her. He had become selfishly filled with anger to the point it had destroyed his relationship with her. Levinia was in mourning too, but he didn't seem to care about *her* loss. She and Daniel were connected, as all twins were, and she'd suffered the loss of a part of herself that she just couldn't explain to anyone—especially when she didn't even understand it herself.

Deciding she should wait until her father fell asleep, Levinia listened carefully for the soft snoring that would let her know her father was down for the night. As the whistles and sputters began to resonate through the house, she relaxed. Only now would she feel safe leaving the *haus* and entering the loft to feed the handsome *Englischer*.

Thankfully, Bethany would soon be gone, and would not return until the wee hours of the morning, leaving Levinia alone with Nate.

Giddiness rose up in her causing her to tremble lightly at the thought of spending time alone with the handsome stranger. She had to admit, though, that if he wasn't injured the way he was, and incapable of overpowering her, she certainly would not spend any time alone with him. In his current state, as an injured man, his dependence on her made him somehow seem *safer* in her eyes. Her father would certainly disagree if he knew about Nate's presence in their home, but if she could help it, he would *never* discover her secret.

Trusting Bethany with the secret was a whole other story, and she was not ready to face *that* fight that was sure to rear its ugly head soon enough. For now, she would enjoy some time with Nate without the threat of her sister betraying her.

Levinia balanced the tray with a large bowl of stew and extra buttermilk biscuits, along with a pitcher of fresh lemonade as she climbed the stairs to the loft. Before she even reached the top step, she could hear her sister giggling and flirting with Nate. She steadied the tray and listened for a moment. She was not happy to hear that her sister was alone with the *Englischer*.

Jealousy rose up in her. Why must she compete with her younger sister for everything? It just wasn't fair. Bethany came by her beauty honestly; she was the lucky one that closely resembled their mother. Levinia, on the other hand, could pass for her brother if she donned a pair of trousers and a straw hat, and cut her hair. She just didn't stand a chance if her sister got in her way.

It would seem Bethany intended to do just that.

"I hope you don't think I'm rude," Nate said. "But I'm too tired for company tonight."

You tell her, Nate!

"I promise I won't stay long," Bethany begged.

Can't you take a hint, dear schweschder?

"If you don't mind, I'd like to get some rest so I don't have to burden your family for too long."

"You're not a burden at all, Nate. In fact, I'm glad you're here. You're a refreshing change from the immature boys in the community."

Stop throwing yourself at him so shamelessly, little schweschder!

"Please, Miss…"

"Bethany. *Mei* name is Bethany."

Levinia couldn't help but giggle at her sister's tone. She was obviously irritated he'd forgotten her name.

"Surely you understand, *Bethany,* that I need my rest so I can be up and on my feet as soon as possible. I have a job waiting for me that I am unable to do unless I get the rest I need to heal. If I can't work, I won't be able to support myself."

"*N-Nee,*" Bethany stuttered. "I understand. Do you need anything before I go?"

Please say no, please say no!

"Uh, no. Thank you. I'll see you tomorrow."

"Goodnight, then."

"Goodnight, uh…"

"Bethany!"

"Right. Goodnight, Bethany."

Good night dear schweschder!

Bethany nearly ran Levinia over as she exited the screen door. She clenched the tray to keep from wearing the contents as Bethany brushed by her without saying a word. She stomped down each step angrily, while Levinia suppressed the urge to laugh at her sister's tantrum. She was obviously put out by Nate rejecting her offer to keep him company.

To Bethany, it was a crisis, but to Levinia, it was an opportunity.

CHAPTER 6

Levinia stood outside the screen door, trying to work up the nerve to enter the loft after overhearing Nate ask her sister to leave. For a moment, she debated whether she should enter or not, but then she remembered he'd asked for the stew. She regretted taking so long in getting his supper to him—perhaps he was now too tired to eat it.

If he's not up to having company, I'll leave the tray with him and go home then.

Anticipating the squeak of the screen door before she opened it, she tried pulling slowly on the handle, but that only made it worse.

"Who's there?" Nate called from the bedroom.

"I'm bringing your supper," Levinia said as she stepped inside the small kitchen. "May I come in?"

"Please do," he begged. "I'm starving!"

Levinia was happy to hear that at least her stew was welcome. Time would tell if Nate would welcome her company for any longer than it took to serve him the stew. As she entered the small bedroom, Nate tried to sit himself up in the bed, but was failing miserably.

"Smells heavenly, but I'm afraid you might have to stay and help me eat it. I'm not sure if I can sit up enough to feed myself!"

Levinia's heart did a somersault behind her ribcage. She relished the idea of spoon-feeding this man more than she probably ought to. She set the tray on the bedside table while she took note of Nate's struggle to gain a semi-sitting position without hurting himself.

"Let me help you," she offered.

He took the hand she offered. "Thank you, Levinia."

Her gaze locked with his only for a moment, but it was long enough to see kindness in his eyes. But there was something else. Something that drew her into them. Something that resembled *love.*

He remembered mei name!

Only moments ago, he'd forgotten her sister's name—or had he? Had he *forgotten* as a means to get rid of her? Levinia certainly hoped it was so.

She couldn't help but smile as she continued to gaze into Nate's eyes.

He cleared his throat. "I'm ready."

Levinia felt warmth radiating from her spine to her cheeks. She was certain her face had turned several shades of red as embarrassment coursed through her.

"I'm sorry. Um—I'll just—well, here. Let me put this napkin under your—chin."

Levinia fumbled with the linen trying to place it in the vicinity of his neckline without touching him. She didn't understand how she could suddenly be so terrified to touch him. She wanted desperately to crawl into the crook of his arm and sink into him, but the fear of rejection eclipsed her desire.

Nate gently pulled her hand into his, guiding her shaky fingers to set the linen napkin into place. Her hand fit nicely in his, and she allowed his grasp to linger over hers.

"Is something troubling you?"

His question startled her, causing her to yank her hand away.

"*Nee*—no. I'm just a little tired is all."

She would never admit to the sudden tension she felt around him that stemmed from attraction to him.

"I think I detect a little worry in your beautiful, green eyes."

What? He thinks I have beautiful eyes!

Deep down, Levinia knew better than to put any stock in such prideful compliments. *Ach,* she suddenly didn't care. Being humble and proper hadn't gotten her anywhere in life except lonely and alone. If this *Englischer* wanted to take her away from all that, even if only for the duration of his stay in the loft, she would gladly encourage him!

"*Nee,* not worry, but perhaps a little apprehension. You are an *Englischer,* and you speak more boldly than I'm used to."

She thinks I'm an Englischer! Should I tell her the truth?

"Don't tell me none of your other *boyfriends* ever paid you a compliment."

"I've not had time for dating. *Mei mamm* passed away just before *mei* tenth birthday. *Mei schweschder*--sister, Bethany was only four at the time. I've been like a momma to her, and I've taken care of *mei daed* and twin *bruder*—brother up until he died two years ago."

Levinia hung her head with sadness at the mention of Daniel.

Nate put his fingers under her chin and lifted until her eyes locked on his adoring gaze. "It seems to me it's time to start taking care of *you.*"

"Amish are not the same as *Englischers.* We take *familye* responsibility very serious. I have a duty to *mei daed* and *schweschder.*"

"Seems to me your sister is grown, and a bit selfish and immature, if I may speak boldly. As for your dad, he isn't incapable of caring for his own needs. What would they do if you married?"

"I don't think that would ever happen. But in those situations, an Amish husband would help me to care for *mei familye.*"

"What if *I* wanted to marry you?"

Levinia felt her heart slam against her ribs. "I assume you ask that for the sake of argument?"

Nate shrugged. "What if I was serious?"

Levinia reached up and prodded the knot on his head. "Perhaps you hit your head harder than I originally thought. You must be suffering from a concussion. How is your vision? Is it blurry?"

"There is nothing wrong with my vision— but I wouldn't mind seeing double. Two of you would be quite nice!"

Levinia sighed playfully. "Will you be serious for just a minute?"

"I am being serious!" he scoffed. "Life is too short to hold your tongue when you have something important to say. I'd consider myself lucky to be able to marry a woman like you."

"A woman like *me*? What do you mean by that?"

He reached up and stroked her cheek. "The sort of woman who is beautiful—inside and out."

Levinia tucked her chin shyly, but Nate lifted it with his fingers until her gaze met his again.

"Why would you want to marry me? We are from two different worlds. Besides, you've only just met me!"

"We aren't so different, you and me. But first, answer something for me; what do you suppose your family would do without you here to serve them?"

Levinia giggled as she pondered his question. "I suppose they would probably starve to death wearing dirty clothes!"

"That is exactly my point. Don't you think you should teach them to fend for themselves? You can't be a servant to them for the rest of their lives. *You* deserve to have a life too."

"By marrying you?" she asked jokingly.

He took her hand in his and kissed the back of it. "Why not?"

She snatched her hand away. "Because unless you're Amish, then *mei daed* will never allow it."

He used her hand to draw her close to him.

"What about what *you* want?"

She splayed her hand over his chest, enjoying the feel of his warm skin and the curly hairs beneath her fingers just before she pushed away from him. "It doesn't matter what I want. It only matters that I follow the rules of the Ordnung."

Nate crossed his arms over his chest defiantly.

"That is exactly why I left."

"What's exactly…" she paused to look him over once more before finishing her sentence. "Wait—you're Amish, aren't you?"

"*Jah,*" he admitted. "But until I met you, I knew exactly what I was going to do."

Levinia wasn't certain if she was overjoyed that he was indeed Amish, or angry that he'd kept the truth from her. She supposed all that mattered was that he finally told her.

"And what is that supposed to mean?"

"I was planning on hiding out at *mei* cousin, Adam's, farm until the harvest was over. I figured that would give me enough time to see if I was ready for the baptismal classes—to make a decision if I was going to stay or go to live among the *Englisch.*"

"What does any of that have to do with me?"

He took her hands in his and gently caressed them. "Because until I met you, I had mostly decided I would leave. But now I would like to stay and court you, especially if the possibility of marrying you exists."

"Surely you've had other opportunities in your own community."

She silently chided herself the minute the words left her mouth, but she needed to know if he was serious.

"*Jah,*" he admitted. "There were plenty of opportunities handed to me, but none that I cared to accept."

Levinia pushed down the giddiness that tried to overtake her. "Why would you want to court me instead of someone like—someone like *mei schweschder?*"

Why can't I keep from putting mei foot in mei mouth?

Nate squeezed her hands fondly. "I've had my fill of offers from selfish, spoiled girls like Bethany. I want a *fraa* who will put me first, just as I would put *her* first. I want a beautiful, giving woman—like *you.*"

CHAPTER 7

Levinia stood abruptly, allowing her gaze to focus on Nate's bare chest. "I'm not certain we should be here alone—without an escort. If you are serious about courting, *mei daed* will never agree to it if he thinks we've acted improperly."

"The girls in my own community in Ohio put a light in their windows at night, and the guys come around and take them courting in their buggies until the wee hours of the morning. Don't they do the same here?"

"*Jah,* Bethany leaves the *haus* nearly every night. She is a wild one. If *mei daed* were to ever find out, he would not approve, but I make excuses for her behavior and cover for her."

Nate caught Levinia staring at him, and tucked his hand in hers. "You haven't told me if you would consent to being courted by me."

Levinia blew out a discouraging sigh. "You've only just met me. You don't really know enough about me yet to make that kind of decision."

He squeezed her hand. "I know all I need to know about you. I heard the kind words from you when you rescued me, and the prayers you said for me. You are a humble servant who has been taken advantage of by your *familye*. Perhaps *you* are the one in need of rescuing."

Levinia couldn't help but agree with him, but she would never admit to such a thing. In as much as she would enjoy this *mann's* company, she could not accept his proposal of courting—especially if it could lead to marriage. She had an obligation to her *daed* and Bethany, and to the memory of her dear *bruder,* Daniel.

Nate tucked his hand under her chin and lifted gently to set her gaze back on him. "What has you so worried? Is it because you don't know *mei familye?* I will be happy to introduce you to *mei* cousin, Adam. I think we are close to the Troyer farm, *jah?*"

Levinia stiffened. She *knew* Nate. He hadn't visited their community in some years, but she remembered him. Adam was friends with Daniel, and the three of them spent an entire summer working the neighboring farms after the big hail storm that took out the early crops. There was a lot of replanting that year. Working bees had kept Levinia busy with the women in the community to keep the working men from going hungry.

Nate smiled. "You're thinking of the hail storm. I do remember catching fireflies at dusk and sipping lemonade that a certain young lady made for me."

"I made it for the *menner* who were working to replant the fields."

Nate pushed out his lips and smiled. "My mouth is still all puckered up from that tart lemonade given to me by the prettiest girl in the whole county."

Nate pulled her close and placed his puckered lips against hers.

Caught off guard, Levinia was too stunned to return the kiss. The next one, however, she eagerly took pleasure in.

He deepened the kiss, consuming her with his every breath. His impulsive passion seemed to employ a responsive urgency in her. He wanted her—every bit of her.

Levinia's flighty heartbeat didn't interfere with her insatiable hunger for Nate's sweet, warm kisses. All thoughts focused on the feel of his lips against her mouth, her cheeks, and her neck. It was making her dizzy with delight, but she was powerless to stop him—not that she wanted to. She was ready to give herself to this man who made her feel more alive than she'd felt her entire life. She was a part of him already, and no ghosts of the past could separate them.

❧❦

Bethany washed down the last bite of snitz pie with a big gulp of milk as she watched angrily from the kitchen window for her older sister to leave the loft.

What is she doing up there?

More than half an hour had passed since Bethany had brushed by Levinia as she'd exited the small living space above the barn where they'd hidden the handsome *Englischer.*

He *was* handsome.

And Bethany had her intention set on him.

She tapped her foot against the wooden floor, becoming angrier with each tap.

How long would she wait for Levinia to exit the loft?

Another possibility suddenly crossed her mind. What if he'd hurt her sister? Their *daed* had warned them about trusting *Englischers* too many times to remember.

But Nate was injured.

What if he was faking?

After all, he'd asked *her* to leave, claiming to be too tired for company. Surely he wouldn't be entertaining Levinia—would he? Bethany's anger and jealousy turned full-circle, and recycled itself in her mind, bringing her such angst she couldn't escape the kitchen fast enough. She quickly conquered the distance between the *haus* and the barn, climbing the stairs lightly so as not to alert the *Englischer* and interrupt possible cover-up of his wrongdoing against Levinia.

Bethany fully intended to catch the *Englischer,* but wanted to remain quiet in case her sister was in trouble. The element of surprise could mean the difference between saving Levinia and getting caught in the man's trap along with her sister.

She tiptoed up the last few stairs and peeked inside the screen door.

They were nowhere to be seen.

All was quiet—too quiet.

Bethany's heart beat rapidly at the thoughts that flashed through her mind of Levinia lying dead on the floor while Nate hovered over her with a weapon in his hands. Just because he was handsome didn't mean he wasn't capable of being a dangerous *killer,* did it?

Focus, she chided herself. *Levinia could be in danger.*

Carefully opening the screen door only enough to squeeze through, Bethany was relieved she'd managed to slip through without the hinges creaking. She shook as she padded quietly across the linoleum floor of the small kitchen toward the bedroom door. She paused before looking in the room, momentarily wondering what she would do if she should catch him hurting Levinia.

Lord, help me to save mei schweschder if she should be in trouble. Give me strength to deal with whatever I find behind this door.

Nothing could have prepared Bethany for what she saw as she peered around the doorframe. Too stunned to speak, Bethany stood there observing Nate and Levinia engaged in a steamy sequence of kisses. At first, she wondered if the way he was holding her was possibly against her will, but it was soon evident that Levinia was an all-too-willing participant in the inappropriate scene unfolding before her eyes.

Anger rose up in her. She'd wanted to explore that very option with the handsome *Englischer.* But here was her older sister—her very *plain* older sister gaining the attention from the very man who'd just rejected *her* less than an hour ago.

Jealousy filled her.

What did Levinia have that Bethany didn't have? What did he see in her? She was shaped like a boy, and could easily pass for their brother, Daniel.

Bethany had gained enough attention from the local boys to *know* she was physically desirable. Levinia, on the other hand, had never been on even one date.

What if *that* was the appeal? What if her innocence was what attracted him to her? Perhaps, then, her sister was indeed in danger of being compromised by this *Englischer*. She had to put a stop to his plot against Levinia before he compromised her.

She cleared her throat, but neither of them stopped mauling each other.

Clearing her throat again, she shuffled toward them, making them aware of her presence.

Levinia jumped up from the edge of the bed, leaving the shirtless *Englischer* feverishly wiping his mouth in her wake. Holding her hands up to her obviously angry sister, Levinia sent Bethany a pleading look.

"I can explain," she quickly offered.

Bethany pursed her lips. "What is there to explain? I clearly saw this stranger—this *Englischer* taking advantage of you!"

"That's not true," he said in his defense. "I'm not a stranger, and I've asked Levinia if I can court her."

Bethany took an aggressive step toward Nate and gritted her teeth at him. "It sounds to me like you've done this before. Courting Levinia? You really expect her to believe such lies? You saw her as a vulnerable opportunity—nothing else. I'd be willing to bet you make a habit of taking advantage of innocent girls!"

"You're right. Because this isn't the first time I've broken a few ribs and gotten lucky enough to be stowed away on an Amish farm by an unsuspecting woman such as Levinia!" he scorned her. "Listen to how *narrish* you sound."

Bethany gasped. "And now you mock us by using the Amish language against us?"

Nate was growing impatient with Bethany's accusations. "I used the word because I *am* Amish!"

Bethany looked at Levinia to confirm the lie he was telling. Right on cue, she defended him.

Bethany turned and walked toward the door. "I don't want to hear any more of these lies. I'm getting *Daed.* Surely *he* will settle this—*mann-to-mann!"*

CHAPTER 8

Levinia chased after Bethany as she ran down the steps that led to the loft. The screen door slammed behind her, and she worried Nate would think her to be uncivilized for her abrupt reaction to her sister's threat. When she caught up with Bethany, Levinia looped her fingers in the crook of her sister's arm, forcing her to stop running from her. "I'm not going to tolerate the disrespect you've shown me any longer. You are nothing short a spoiled *boppli* and I won't allow you to threaten me. If you want to tell *daed,* I'll be telling him what *you* do every night when you sneak out of the *haus.*"

Bethany pulled in a breath and narrowed her eyes. "You wouldn't dare!"

Levinia grabbed Bethany's arm and began to pull her toward the kitchen door. "Let's go tell *daed* everything and then we'll both fall under the ban!"

Bethany began to cry. "Please don't tell. I don't want to be shunned. I can't take care of myself out there in that big world without you and *daed* to take care of me. You're right! I've been acting spoiled for a while now—since about the same time Daniel went to Heaven. I didn't think you cared about me anymore because you're always so moody."

Levinia pulled Bethany into her arms. "Of course I still care about you! All we seem to have anymore is each other. Since *Daed* lost Daniel, he won't forgive me for not saving him, and that has made me feel sad."

Bethany sniffled. *"Daed* doesn't blame you. It wasn't your fault. You called for an ambulance. You did everything you could to stop the bleeding, but *Gott* reached down from Heaven and took him from us."

"*Daed* doesn't see it that way. He doesn't even look at me anymore, and he barely speaks to me. I think he stopped loving me."

"*Ach,* Levinia, he still loves you. Don't talk like that. I think he's just sad is all."

Levinia hung her head. "He doesn't forgive me any more than I forgive myself. I shouldn't have called that ambulance. I panicked. All that blood…"

Her breath caught in her throat and she suppressed a strangled sob. "I didn't mean to let him or *Daed* down. I wish I could have taken Daniel's place. *Daed* would have been better off."

Bethany grabbed Levinia by the arms and gave her a gentle shake. "Don't you ever let me hear you talk like that again! I don't know what I would do without you."

"You don't care about me any more than *Daed* does. You both take me for granted and take advantage of *mei gut* nature."

Bethany let go of Levinia's arms and pulled her into a hug. "I'm sorry I've let you take all the responsibility around here. I promise I'll learn how to cook and all the other things I ain't *gut* at."

Levinia sniffled. "I love you, dear *schweschder.*"

Bethany gave Levinia a squeeze. "I love you too. I'm sorry I don't say that to you often enough."

Wiping her tears, Levinia looked into Bethany's eyes with a seriousness she'd never shown before.

Bethany waved a hand at her and scoffed.

"Don't worry. I ain't gonna tell *Daed* about Nate, but I gotta know; is he *really* Amish?"

"*Jah,* he's Adam Troyer's cousin."

Bethany waggled her eyebrows. "So you *really* are going to court him then?"

Levinia shrugged. "I don't have time, and besides, I'd feel guilty."

"Those kisses I witnessed didn't look like they were full of guilt. What do you have to feel guilty over? *Daed* and I can take care of ourselves."

Levinia shrugged.

"What is it, dear, *schweschder?"*

"I would feel bad going on with my life and being happy when...when Daniel can't enjoy his life anymore. He'll never get married or have *kinner,* so why should I be able to?"

Bethany furrowed her brow with concern. "He may never get married or have *kinner,* but he's in Heaven. He's not missing out on life. Maybe he's missing it on this earth, but he has eternal life now. He's not unhappy, and he wouldn't want *you* to be unhappy either."

Levinia smiled. "When did you get to be so wise?"

"Because *you* raised me!"

They both giggled and Levinia pulled Bethany into a sincere hug. "I'm sorry for the things I said to you—about you being spoiled."

"You shouldn't apologize for telling the truth. I *have* been acting spoiled. I've let you do all the work around here, and that hasn't been fair to you. I'm sorry for that. I'll try harder from now on."

Levinia blew out a sigh of relief. "That would be *wunderbaar!"*

"So what are you going to do about Nate?"

Levinia shrugged. "I don't know what I should do."

Bethany laughed. "When a *mann* that handsome asks to court you—you give him your consent!"

"But..."

"Don't make excuses, Levinia. He looked serious about you. And you deserve to be happy. Don't worry about *Daed;* I'll take care of him for a change. In the meantime, go to Nate and tell him you will consent to courting him. If you don't, someone else will. He's a handsome catch."

Levinia knew in her mind that it was the logical and right thing to do—for the sake of her future. This was her chance to really be happy, and Bethany was right about Daniel. He would want her to be happy. Nate certainly made her feel like the happiest woman in the entire county—maybe even the history of mankind—if such a thing was possible.

Giggling with giddiness, Levinia turned around and started toward the stairs to the loft. She turned and paused to wink at her sister.

"Go and be happy—promise me you'll be happy."

Levinia smiled brightly. "I intend to."

Levinia made fast tracks to the stairs that led to her future—a future filled with happiness with a very handsome, Amish *mann* who wanted to court *her*.

CHAPTER 9

Levinia stepped into the room where her potential *betrothed* lay snoring lightly. She gently placed her hand upon Nate's bare chest, feeling the gentle rhythm of his heart that beat in perfect tempo with her own. She couldn't help but smile as he covered her hand with his, but remained asleep. She definitely wanted this man. She wanted every part of him. But in the back of her mind, all she could hear were her father's reprimands the day of Daniel's death. The very reprimands that filled her with too much guilt to live her life to its fullest potential.

Though she tried to block out his angry words, she couldn't help but drift back to that dreadful day…

Levinia hung precariously over the top of the split-rail fence watching her twin *bruder* repair the barbed wire at the top of the chicken pen.

"Look at that one, Daniel," Levinia squealed. "It looks like a *mann* holding an umbrella—with a big roaring lion ready to leap out at him."

Daniel took his attention off his work and looked up into the sky to humor his twin. "They just look like clouds to me, but if you say so, then I believe you can see *things* in those clouds."

"You have to use your imagination, dear *bruder.*"

Daniel took another look. He couldn't bear to disappoint his sister. "Well since I'm older—and wiser than you are, I'll leave the imagining to *you.*"

"*Ach,* you are only older by twelve minutes! That doesn't automatically make you wiser."

Daniel tightened the wire and connected the end to assure the chickens stayed *in* and the foxes stayed *out.* "Of course it does. I'm too old to indulge in silly *girl* games of watching the clouds. Don't you have some laundry to hang on the line?"

Levinia sighed. "If I didn't know better, I'd think you were trying to get rid of me."

"That's *narrish.* I wouldn't dream of trying to get rid of my favorite twin!"

Levinia furrowed her brow. "You say that all the time, but you know I'm your *only* twin."

Daniel chuckled. "That's why you're *mei* favorite!"

"*Nee,* you patronize me!"

"Don't let *Daed* hear you using big words like that or he'll know about those unapproved books you've got hiding in the loft."

Levinia gasped. "How did you know about those books?"

"I know more than you think I do."

"And you haven't told *Daed?* "

"*Nee,* I figured if he found out he'd put you under the ban, and I, for one, would not be able to live even one day without listening to your musings. They keep me grounded where I belong."

Levinia lifted her head, feeling a little woozy as the blood rushed back to her brain all at once after hanging upside down for so long. "What do you mean?"

"You don't think I've wondered what life would be like out there—in the world? I've flipped through a few of those books myself, and though I found nothing wrong with the content, the Elders and *Daed* would see it differently."

He could see he had Levinia's full attention, and momentarily wondered if he should continue to talk about such a risky subject.

"I've got an obligation to this *familye* as the eldest son, and that's a big responsibility. You and Bethany have the advantage of leaving the community and searching out another life—away from here, if you should choose to do so."

Levinia's eyes widened with every word her brother spoke. "You've thought of *leaving* too?"

"*Jah,* I have."

There. He'd said it. Now what?

"Let me backtrack a minute for you. Back to before—before *mamm* left us. Life was *gut* then. *Daed* was happy and life on this farm was something special. With *mamm* gone, each year became more and more difficult. Suddenly you were raising Bethany, and I was doing the work of two *menner*. *Daed* shut down and barely functioned for some years. We were only *kinner* at the time and didn't understand, but that kind of life makes a child grow up fast—too fast."

Levinia reflected on his statement, knowing that what he said was painfully true.

"There is a whole world out there to explore, and if all you ever do is experience it through your books, then that is better than the stifling existence we've come to accept here in this community. You can't be Bethany's *mamm* forever. Soon, very soon, you will meet a *mann* who will love you and want to raise a *familye* with you. That is the *familye* you should raise."

Levinia didn't believe a word he was saying. She knew how plain she was. All of her friends had begun courting over a year ago, and some were already married, but she hadn't been asked on one date yet.

"*Ach,* I'll probably end up a spinster."

"If you do it will be the fault of our *daed* who has put the burden of *his* responsibilities on us. I'd like to marry someday too, but I doubt it will happen for me. You and Bethany have a chance to marry if I am the one who stays to take care of *Daed.* If *Daed* would have accepted help from the community as he should have, or even remarried for our sake, then you would have had a real childhood and so would I have. We would have had normal chores of a farm, and been able to enjoy our growing years instead of having the responsibility of taking on the role of *parent* to our *daed* and a *boppli* at such an early age."

"But even I know how much *Daed* missed *mamm*. He still does. I hear him talking to her at night when he's praying just before he goes to sleep."

"*Jah,* and I feel bad about that, but as painful as it was for him to accept, he should have been the parent instead of allowing you and me to step into that role."

Levinia tipped her head back again, hoping the distraction of the clouds would put an end to the very serious conversation she and Daniel were having, but it didn't work. "Perhaps if I am the one to stay, then *you* can marry and have a *familye*. *Daed* built the loft for you to live in when you find a *fraa*."

Daniel scoffed. "*Daed* forgot one important thing."

"What's that?"

"Time."

Levinia scrunched up her face. "Time for what?"

Daniel furrowed his brow. "Exactly *mei* point. There is never enough time to live our lives. No time at the end of the day to meet someone, much less to find the time to court."

"We mingle with enough of the youth at work bees and whatnot, but you're right. We haven't been to one Singing despite the many invitations from our friends. Why do we always make excuses instead of just attending one?"

Daniel wiped his dampened brow with the back of his shirtsleeve. The back of his neck was red from the sun, and Levinia knew he was in need of a cool drink soon before he collapsed from the heat. She didn't want to go inside just yet. The clothes on the line still had at least another half an hour before they would dry in the humid, summer heat. She had come to realize Daniel was right about the lack of joy in their everyday lives.

Right at this moment, all she wanted to do was to get lost in the formations of the clouds. She hung upside down again, her grip on the edge of the fence slipping. "Help!"

Daniel stepped toward her, hoping he could catch Levinia and prevent her from toppling to the ground below, but instead, he tripped and fell against the taught, barbed wire fence, his wrist catching a barb. His flesh tore open as he slid to the ground, the pain unbearable. He let out a series of rumbling groans as he struggled to clasp shut the gash he just couldn't see around the uncontrolled flow of blood at his wrist.

Levinia fell backward off the fence rail and landed on her shoulder, hearing a crack accompanied by instant pain when she hit the hard-packed ground below. She rolled to her other side, struggling to regain her footing. Her hand went up to her obviously broken collar bone, her knees felt weak and her stomach heaved from the pain. She could hear Daniel groaning, but momentary disorientation kept her from him.

Levinia finally turned toward Daniel.

Panic filled her at the expanse of blood covering her *bruder* and the soil around him.

Tucking her arm to her side against the pain in her collarbone, Levinia bolted toward Daniel and fell to her knees beside him.

"What do I do?"

Daniel shook and shivered. "You need—to—tie it off—to stop—the bleeding."

Tears filled Levinia's eyes and she shook so violently with fear that she struggled to tear off her apron, the pain of her broken bone making it a struggle. Ripping the hem brought unbearable pain, but she needed to strip the cloth enough to tie off Daniel's bloody wound. With shaky hands, she ignored her own pain and wrapped the heavy linen strip around his wrist three times, knotting the ends over the strip that was already saturated with blood.

"It's not helping," she cried.

Daniel was weak, his eyes turning a hazy grey.

"Go—to the barn—call an—ambulance."

She pushed herself up with one arm and staggered to the barn, her chest heaving with fear.

At her father's work table she picked up the receiver and hit 9-1-1.

"9-1-1, what's your emergency?"

Levinia relayed Daniel's condition and her address all in one sentence, tossing the phone down on the tool bench without bothering to hang up. She stumbled back to the yard where she'd left Daniel, his lifeless form bringing terror to her every step. By the time she reached him, she was numb.

She dropped back to her knees beside him and began tearing another couple of strips of cloth from her apron, tying each piece in vain. Before she could even tie the ends, the blood soaked through the material. She tied another strip above the wound, hoping that would keep the blood from draining too quickly. He might lose his arm from the break in circulation, but at least it would spare his life—wouldn't it?

Daniel looked up at her with an unexplained urgency. "Promise me—that..."

Levinia shook her head madly. "Don't try to talk. Save your energy. I can hear the sirens. They'll be here in just another minute."

Daniel coughed and shook, his ashen features sinking. "Promise me—you'll marry—and have your—own *familye.*"

Tears poured down her cheeks at his words. She didn't want to promise such a thing. She knew what a promise like that meant and she was not ready to give up on her brother's life. The ambulance barreled down the dirt drive toward them.

She could see it.

Her brother would be safe. He was going to be just fine—wasn't he? She looked down at Daniel, his lashes fluttered against a set of eyes that had turned dark. Eyes she no longer recognized. Eyes with barely any life left in them.

She choked back a heavy sob threatening to force its way out.

"Promise—me," he said with a weak urgency.

She reluctantly made the promise, but it was too late.

He was already gone.

The memory of the sirens screaming in the driveway tormented her. If only she'd gotten him that cold drink instead of hanging upside-down over the fence rail. The ambulance had come, but they were too late.

None of it mattered now. She was alive and he was—dead and gone.

Her hand resting against Nate's warm flesh made her replay the promise she'd made to Daniel. She'd promised to marry and have a *familye* of her own.

Was that possible with Nate?

Could she allow Nate to court her knowing it could end in marriage?

Bethany had given her blessing, but what would her *daed* do if she tried to leave his *haus* to cling to Nate? Would he ever give his approval, or would she forever be scorned in his eyes, unworthy of any happiness?

Nate stirred, looking up at her with soft, loving eyes. He pulled her into the crook of his arm, holding her tightly against him. Suddenly, her *daed's* approval no longer mattered, and neither did his harsh words.

CHAPTER 10

Nate reached up and tenderly brushed away a tear from Levinia's cheek—a tear she didn't know was there.

"What has you so upset? Did it go that badly with your *schweschder?*"

Levinia paused to reflect on the very mature conversation she'd had with Bethany. "*Nee,* it went as opposite as it could have. We settled a lot with that argument. Funny, but we'd never argued before—ever."

"Then what is troubling you so much it's caused you to cry?"

Levinia couldn't look at him.

"I was thinking of *mei bruder—mei* twin."

Nate nodded knowingly. *"Ach,* Daniel. I heard of his death from *mei* cousin. The three of us hung around together the summer I stayed to help with the replanting. That's how I knew of *you."*

He picked up her hand and held it to his warm cheek. "I remembered thinking that entire summer that you worked way too hard for a girl your age. You worked alongside the women in the community and never once participated in any of the youth activities. I so wanted you to come out with us just once to a Singing or a bonfire outing, and I even looked for you, but you never showed up. Daniel knew that I liked you then, but he told me you would never give me a second look because you were too serious about your responsibilities. He was right."

Levinia's heart caught in her throat, keeping her from responding. Nate liked her back then? How had she missed that? Daniel had been right about one point he'd made the day of his death; she had become her *mamm* from the time she was just a girl herself.

She sat up and looked him in the eye. "We were fifteen then, why didn't you say something to me?"

He looked into her questioning eyes, her voice choked with emotion.

"I was awkward at that age. It was easier for me to admire you from afar, than to be rejected up close and personal."

Levinia felt sorry about Nate's youthful angst.

"I suppose I most likely would have rejected you then. I was too serious at that age. I felt I had to keep up with the other women in the community as Bethany's "*mamm*" in order for them to take me seriously. I hope you understand."

Nate used her hand to pull her back toward him.

"As long as you don't reject me now, I'll recover."

She wouldn't dream of rejecting him. He was going to be easy to love. She already did love him. It amazed her how much change her heart had gone through in just a few short hours. Her sister had finally decided to grow up and release her from the responsibility of raising her, and Levinia had finally released the burden of guilt she'd been carrying around for the past two years over Daniel's death.

Most importantly were the feelings she'd developed for Nate in such a short time, and the impact those changes in circumstances would bring to her life. She was about to begin living her life, and she'd never felt more free in her spirit.

Levinia looked into Nate's tender, brown eyes. There was love for her in those eyes, and she felt it like the warmth of a sunny day. How did she get to be so lucky?

Then it hit her.

"I'm curious about something…"

He went to kiss her, but she stiffened.

"What is it?"

"Why are you wearing *Englischer's* clothing and why did you let me think you were an *Englischer?*"

"I suppose I was trying it out—in case I decided to leave my community for good. I didn't intend to stay here and I certainly didn't intend on falling in love with you all over again."

"All over again?"

Nate winked at her. "I had it bad for you that summer. I didn't want to leave here without telling you, but Adam talked me out of it."

Levinia looked at him lovingly. "I wish you would have told me."

He smiled, his dimples inviting her to kiss him.

"I wish I would have told you, too. But at least you know now."

"Since you didn't intend on staying here, I can have Bethany go over and let Adam know you are here so he can arrange to take you to his farm to care for you."

He pulled her closer. "Now wait a minute. Don't I have a say in this? I'd much rather *you* take care of me than Adam."

Levinia enjoyed hearing that Nate needed her, and even wanted her to care for him. She liked this vulnerable and needy side to him, and she would be more than happy to pamper him while he stayed.

"I'd like that too. But for now, you need your rest."

Levinia went to get up, but Nate held her playfully.

"Please don't leave yet. Part of the enjoyment of having you take care of me is so I can spend more time with you."

There was longing in his eyes, a longing Levinia was powerless to resist.

"I suppose since we *are* courting now, I can stay for a while."

She propped his pillows behind his head so he could comfortably lean against them in a semi-sitting position. He held out his arm for her to cuddle him.

"I don't want to hurt you if I lean against your ribs."

He smiled. "*Ach,* I'm tough. Besides, I had some ibuprofen in my bag and I took a few when you went after Bethany, so it's started working on the pain. I don't think I cracked any of the ribs. I think they're just bruised."

Levinia sat down gingerly beside him for two reasons; she didn't want to injure him, and she was still a little in shock that this *mann* was *hers.* She giggled inwardly as she cuddled up in the crook of his waiting arm. Each breath she took matched his, as did the giddiness of her heartbeat. If this was a dream, she didn't ever want to wake up. As far as she was concerned, his strong arms and protective love would be all she would need for the rest of her days on this earth. Safety engulfed her in those arms. She thought for sure and for certain she could almost live in those arms.

"Tell me, my sweetheart; have you ever thought of leaving the community?"

Her gaze followed the trail of his body until it rested on his eyes. She couldn't tell him how many times she'd thought of leaving, or how many times she'd set out to leave. Even if she hadn't gotten further than packing her suitcase, she didn't want him to know why.

The reasons only brought shame to her heart, shame for resenting her *mamm* for going to Heaven and leaving her to raise Bethany and care for her father. If Nate discovered the grudge she'd harbored in her heart all these years, he might find her thoughts to be wicked, and she didn't want to say or do anything that would cause him to change his mind about courting her. She'd only just found him, and had just found out he'd cared for her so much in their youth that his feelings easily renewed.

Certainly thoughts such as those were best carried with a person to their grave.

"Doesn't every youth in the communities think of leaving at some point?"

It was all she could say at the moment. She'd since-then changed her mind and had even released her *mamm* from the wrongful grudge she'd had against her, so it was probably for the best if she didn't start off her relationship with Nate on a sour note. Her heart was no longer hardened; he'd even changed her in the short time he'd reentered her life. She wanted to be the sort of woman he could be proud to have at his side for the rest of his life, and if that meant she had to rid herself of all that was not holy, she would ask *Gott* to renew her no matter how painful it might be.

"*Jah,* I suppose they do, but I figured you would probably want to leave a little more than most since you had to be a *mamm* to Bethany, and a servant to your *daed.*"

Levinia lowered her gaze, shame overtaking her. Nate lifted her chin to force her gaze back on him.

"There is no shame in not wanting to be in a role you aren't supposed to be in. I was in a similar spot myself until a few weeks ago when *mei* younger *schweschder* married. *Mei mamm* and *daed* were killed in a buggy accident just over eight years ago, and I was left to finish raising Amanda on my own. I farmed *mei daed's* land and took care of her. She's eighteen now and just married, so I was suddenly all alone in that *haus.* I'm twenty-six years old and don't know what to do with myself. I left a few days ago because I wondered what would become of me at my age."

Levinia had wondered the same thing of herself. She had no idea he'd suffered the same fate she had. She was only three years younger than Nate, but too old not to be considered a spinster by the community.

"I felt resentment, when after a series of miscarriages, *mei mamm* finally had Amanda. She was her entire world because she was so happy to have a second *boppli,* and a girl, no-less. I was already eight years old, and didn't want more *kinner* to have to share *mei* parents with. But that first time she held my hand and said my name, asking if I'd help her milk our cow, I was happy to be her big *bruder.*"

So far, Levinia could relate to everything he was saying. Should she tell him so?

"But then right after the accident, the resentment came back, but this time it brought with it a deep bitterness and anger disguised as mourning for *mei* parent's death. I told myself I would get over it, but the feelings of resentment only deepened, and that terrified me because I loved Amanda very much and didn't want to dislike her. Truth is, I just wanted our old life back, when both my parents were with us and I thought life couldn't get any better. But as time wore on, it all went away, and I accepted my role as caretaker for Amanda, but that didn't mean I didn't still feel cheated out of the life *mei* friends seemed to be enjoying."

Listening to Nate talk filled her with confirmation that her finding him on the bank of Willow Creek was no coincidence. *Gott* had put him in her path for a reason—to have each other to understand and help each other through the pain of losing loved ones, and the burden they shared for having to care for their sisters in place of a parent.

She *had* to tell him.

She knew it would ease both of their pain.

"It's almost like you're telling me my own life story. I understand the feelings you've experienced because I've felt them too. In case you didn't hear the heated argument between Bethany and me, it's almost a mirror image of what you're telling me."

Nate chuckled and pulled her tight against his shoulder. "I heard the two of you arguing and that's why I'm telling you all of this. We can help each other through our feelings, even though coming here has already changed a lot for me. When Amanda married, I felt more relief than I have for years. I thought to myself *finally, I can get away from all this and live my life the way I want to.* But now that I'm here with you, I realize that distance was not what I need to heal; it was *you.*"

Tears filled Levinia's eyes and she didn't wipe them away before they warmed Nate's shoulder. She listened to the beat of his heart that matched her own.

"I believe we were meant for each other," was all she could say, but it was enough for them both to know there would never be a truer statement.

CHAPTER 11

The cricket's song lulled Nate into deep relaxation, but it was Levinia's company that soothed his weary soul. This was the life for him, not a troubled existence among the *Englisch*. He certainly hadn't been thinking straight when he'd left his farm in Ohio, but now that he'd reunited with Levinia, he was glad he had.

A warm breeze blew in from the open window and played with the blond waves that had escaped Levinia's *kapp*. He delighted in the feel of her in his arms as if she was always meant to be there. He could get used to this. It was the easiest thing in his life in so many years, and he already couldn't imagine his life without her.

She shifted in his arms, her breathing slowed. She had fallen asleep. Though he hated the idea, he would have to wake her soon in order to avoid the appearance of improper behavior. If he wanted to get the blessing of the Elders and her *daed* to marry her, he would have to keep things between them on an approved level.

He pressed his face in her hair and breathed in the smell of lavender and oatmeal. He recognized the scent as being the same blend of natural ingredients his *mamm* used to make homemade soap. He'd continued to use her recipe to make it for himself, but he preferred the plain oatmeal—especially for shaving. His sister, Amanda, used to pick the flowers from their *mamm's* garden so she could add them to her soap to make it a little more feminine, but he never liked it—until now. Smelling it in Levinia's hair put a warm feeling in him he didn't ever want to lose.

చ•ల

Levinia stirred, looking up at Nate, who slept soundly next to her. She felt momentarily anxious at the reality that she'd fallen asleep in Nate's arms. She hadn't meant to, but she was so exhausted from the previous day's chores and the excitement of her new courtship with Nate that she'd suffered a lapse in judgment.

If he wasn't so comfortable and trustworthy, she'd have probably used more caution, never letting her guard down. But now it was nearly dawn, and her *daed* would be expecting his morning meal. She didn't want to leave Nate, but if she didn't slip back to the main *haus* soon, her father would catch her, and that would certainly be the end to her life in the community.

She lifted herself from the crook of Nate's arm, kissed him gently on the cheek and padded her way out of the loft. Being careful to keep the hinges of the screen door from squeaking so the noise wouldn't wake her *boyfriend—betrothed,* she stepped out onto the top step of the small porch and into the cold, morning air.

It was almost November, and the near-wintry breeze that ruffled the hem of her dress made her shiver with the reality of the change in season. No longer would she enjoy the hot days of Indian summer, but she now had the warmth of a new love to keep the chill from her. But in his immediate absence, all she could think about was putting on a pot of hot *kaffi* to warm her outsides to better match her insides.

Levinia headed down the stairs of the loft with caution, being aware that her father could be anywhere this time of the day. The sun cast only enough twilight to light her way to the *haus*. Normally by this time, her father was tucked away safely in the barn busy with the morning milking. If caught, she could reasonably dash toward the chicken coop to make him think she was out to gather the eggs for an early start to the morning meal.

Thankfully, she managed to make her way to the kitchen unseen, where the smell of baking banana bread filled her senses. Panic rose up in her until she spotted Bethany inside the pantry with a load of canned apples, flour and various spices in her arms.

"What are you making, little *schweschder?*"

Bethany blew at a tendril of sandy-brown hair that trickled over her forehead, her stained apron making her look as if she'd stayed up all night cooking.

"*Ach,* I'm going to make an apple pie for the evening meal. I've already started breakfast. I thought I'd try my hand at doing your job since I'm going to have to once you and Nate are married."

Levinia giggled. "You're getting ahead of yourself, Bethany. We haven't officially begun to court yet, so we won't be getting married *this* wedding season. But I do appreciate the effort."

Bethany slumped against the doorframe of the pantry. "You mean I did all this for nothing?"

Levinia crossed the kitchen floor and relieved Bethany of the burden in her arms before she dropped everything and there was a mess for her to clean.

"It wasn't for nothing. Learning to cook is *never* for nothing. It is a skill that all Amish women must master in order to make them an eligible catch for the best *mann* in the community."

Bethany blew out a discouraging sigh. "You got the best *mann* in the community. I've dated all the rest, and believe me, they don't even compare. I've considered giving up on the *menner* in this community."

Levinia's eyes widened. "*You,* give up on dating? Do you feel alright little *schweschder?*"

"*Ach,* don't tease me. I'll have you know that I stayed home last night because I was so discouraged."

Levinia set the food down on the counter and put the back of her hand to Bethany's forehead in jest.

"*Ach,* this *is* serious. You don't even have a fever!"

Bethany swatted Levinia's hand away. "This is serious. Don't make fun of me. I'm worried I'm going to end up a spinster."

Levinia smirked knowingly. "Up until a day ago, I was worried about the same thing. But you shouldn't worry. I *never* thought my life could change so fast, but this just goes to show you that you never know when *Gott* is going to choose to bless you."

Bethany rolled her eyes. "I've managed to find fault with each of the *menner* in this community. Where am I going to find another *mann* as wonderful as you've found?"

Levinia smiled as her thoughts turned to the change in Nate from lying on the bank of Willow Creek unconscious, to so lovingly cradling her in his arms all night. "I *did* just sort of *find* him, didn't I?"

Bethany frowned. "I'm happy for you, but you can wipe the smile from your lips when you're around me, because I'm just not happy."

Levinia took a stainless steel mixing bowl from the cupboard and began the pie crust. "You don't need a *mann* to make you happy. We make our *own* happiness in this world."

Bethany handed her the butter and salt. "That's easy for you to say since you *have* a *mann.*"

Levinia sighed with worry. "I don't have him yet. You've forgotten that *Daed* hasn't given his approval yet."

"You are well beyond the age of approval, Levinia. Besides, you'll be lucky if you get more than a grunt out of him."

"Thank you for calling me old, little *schweschder.*"

"*Ach,* is that all you heard? Me calling you old?"

Bethany began to shake a fair amount of salt into the crust mixture, and Levinia couldn't stop her before it was too late. "Now I have to throw this batch away and start all over again. The recipe calls for just a pinch of salt. How many times have I shown you how to make a pie crust?"

Bethany hung her head. "I'm sorry. But couldn't you just make two crusts and then we won't have to throw it away."

Levinia thought for a minute. "I suppose if we double the recipe, we can make apple turnovers instead. But you will have to take the extras with you when you go to visit the Troyer farm to let them know Nate is here and that he's going to recover here with us."

Bethany furrowed her brow. "That's sort of risky, don't you think? If *Daed* finds him in the loft, we will have a *lot* of explaining to do."

Levinia added more flour and butter to the bowl, her arm already aching from the blending. "That is what Nate and I decided. He will stay with us until he recovers. It will give us a chance to get a head start on our courting."

"When do you plan on presenting it to *Daed?* How are you going to explain how you already know each other?"

Levinia hadn't thought that out.

"I suppose he will come over with Adam after he's recovered and we will play it off as if we've just met. He can ask *Daed* then. Or—we will do like most of the youth and see each other secretly, and *Daed* will never have to know until we are ready to be published for our wedding."

Bethany laughed. "Now that's taking things *way* too far."

"Perhaps," Levinia agreed. "But I'm not even certain any of it will matter, as *Daed* doesn't acknowledge me anyway. I might even have to get married without him present."

Bethany's eyes bulged. "You wouldn't!"

Levinia dropped the fork in the bowl and focused a serious gaze on her sister. "Perhaps I need to shock him into ending his bout of ignoring me."

Bethany shook her head and pursed her lips.

"Don't let him ruin this for you. If it was me, I'd do what was right and *gut* for *mei* future with the *mann* I was destined to marry. *Gott* brought him to you, and you shouldn't let this life get in your way."

Levinia resumed cutting the butter into the flour, recalling inwardly the last conversation she'd had with Daniel. "I practically promised the same thing to our dear *bruder* just before he let go and let *Gott* take him to the great farm in the sky."

Bethany nodded knowingly. "That's a promise I aim to help you keep."

CHAPTER 12

Levinia watched in shock as her *daed* made a show of spitting out his first bite of banana bread into his napkin. He looked up sternly, disapproval furrowing his brow. It was the first time he'd looked directly into Levinia's eyes since Daniel's death.

The look in his eyes terrified Levinia.

"What's wrong with this bread, *dochder?*"

He hadn't called her by her given name in two years. The tone of his voice sent shivers of emotion through her.

"Is there something wrong with it?"

"It tastes like you rubbed it on the underside of a skunk." His deep baritone filled the small kitchen with anger.

Levinia and Bethany each lifted their slice of the bread to their mouths and took a daring nibble while their father watched with much anticipation. They immediately tucked their napkins beneath their lips to catch the vile-tasting bread.

Levinia jumped up from the table nervously, snatching the bread from each plate and taking it to the counter. She quickly grabbed biscuits from the pantry and tossed them into the still-warm oven. "These biscuits will take no time to warm, *Daed.* I'm sorry about the bread. The buttermilk must have gone sour and I didn't realize it."

Bethany stood up abruptly, her chair crashing to the floor behind her. "Why do you cover for me like that, dear *schweschder?"* She turned to her father. "I am the one who made the bread, and I did it to help Levinia who works too hard on this farm, and I…"

He pounded his fist on the table, interrupting her tantrum.

"Silence, *Dochder!*"

Her father's voice rumbled in her, rattling her to her very core. It was the first time he'd referred to *her* so informally. He'd been that way toward Levinia for the past two years, and now, he'd included Bethany in his raging disassociation.

Bethany's face turned up, anger flaring in her eyes. "I was only trying to help."

She threw down her napkin and walked toward the kitchen door. "Nothing is *gut* enough for you is it?"

Levinia watched in shock as Bethany let the screen door slam behind her. She swallowed the lump of fear clogging her throat while her gaze travelled to her father. He was busy shoveling the remainder of his eggs in his mouth as if nothing happened, but she could see lines of distress etched in his permanently stressed face.

Pulling the warm biscuits from the oven, she crossed the room and set the plate in front of her father without looking at him. She feared if she made eye-contact with him again it could only have the worst of consequences for her. As for Bethany, she was certain her father would overlook her tantrum as always and not speak of it again. He'd lost control of his *familye;* that much was now evident to Levinia. How that would affect her impending courtship with Nate remained to be seen. For now, she would carry on with him as planned, and be certain to keep it from her father at all cost.

Levinia removed Bethany's plate from the table and set it on the counter. She reached for her own plate next, hoping her father wouldn't notice, but he startled her by grabbing her arm. He kept his head down toward his own plate, but after a few seconds of discomfort, he let go of her arm and resumed shoveling the last of his eggs onto his fork.

"Leave it. Sit and finish your meal."

Levinia was afraid to sit, and she was afraid to defy her father as Bethany had more times than she could count. Levinia had never stood up to her father. Why did her sister have more courage than she did? She envied her sister for that much, but she supposed she lacked the confidence needed for that sort of courage. Levinia had never been that confident. But with Nate in her life now, she was determined that she would start.

‎❧•❦

When her father finally rose from his chair and exited the kitchen, Levinia blew out a sigh of relief. Within minutes, Bethany whirl-winded into the kitchen and grabbed her plate off the counter, snatching a biscuit from the plate and stuffing most of it in her mouth.

"I thought he'd never leave."

Levinia scowled at Bethany as crumbs spewed from her lips and onto the table. She swatted playfully into the air.

"Don't you have any manners?"

Bethany shook her head while making a show of the chewed-up biscuit in her mouth.

"*Ach,* little *schweschder,* act like a lady."

Bethany rolled her eyes. "You should take your own advice!"

Levinia began to run water in the sink to wash the dishes. "What is that supposed to mean?"

Bethany wriggled her eyebrows. "It means that I had to start the meal this morning because *someone* stayed out all night with her new beau in the loft!"

Levinia could feel the heat of embarrassment rising up her neck and resting on her cheeks. "Speaking of Nate, I should get some food out to him. He needs to keep up his strength."

"I saw *Daed* hitching up the buggy to go into town, so you should be clear to take food up there in about half an hour. You could probably have enough time to visit with Nate before *Daed* returns for the noon meal."

Levinia picked her hands up out of the soapy dishwater and flashed Bethany a pleading look. "Do you mind?"

Bethany let out a heavy sigh, throwing the back of her hand to her forehead. "First I have to cook, and now I have to wash dishes!"

Levinia grabbed a linen dishtowel and dried her hands, twisting the towel and swatting at Bethany with it. "Don't be so dramatic. If you do the dishes, I can finish the apple turnovers."

Bethany jumped up from the table eagerly, bringing her empty plate to the sink and dumping it in the water. "You have got yourself a deal. I will take washing dishes over cooking and baking every time!"

Levinia began to cut the rolled out dough into squares, placing them on the cookie sheet. "You will have to learn some day."

"*Jah,* but I will never measure up to our *mamm.* But you're *gut* enough to run *mamm's* old bakery. Why haven't you ever done that? It just sits out there by the main road all boarded up like an abandoned old shack."

Levinia whipped her head around, piercing Bethany with a discouraging glare. "Don't you remember why *Daed* boarded up the place?"

Bethany shook her head.

Levinia lowered her head, a far-off gaze overtaking her. "I remember that day like it was yesterday. He caught us out there playing, and I'd started a fire in the stove. It was just before *mei* ninth birthday, but I knew what I was doing when it came to *mamm's* bakery. It was only a few weeks after she'd gone to Heaven, but no one ever cleaned out the place, and there was still flour and such in the cellar. I'd brought butter and eggs from the *haus* and decided I was going to make a batch of cookies. When *Daed* saw the smoke rising from the chimney, he'd come running from the fields thinking the place was on fire. But when he discovered us in there baking, he threw it all away and put out the fire in the stove, and then put us out in the yard. He didn't say a word, but I knew when he began to pull the planks of wood from the porch and used them to board up the doors and windows that he was mad."

Bethany stood there washing the same cup over and over again, her full attention on Levinia's story.

"Well by the time *Daed* finished hammering, I'd wet *mei* pants, but you threw a rock at the window and cracked it."

Bethany laughed. "I remember that!"

Levinia finished placing a dollop of apple preserves on each square of dough, and then draped a square over the top and crimped the edges with a fork.

"I don't know how you remember that; you were barely four years old."

Bethany handed Levinia the sugar and went back to scrubbing the pots and pans. Levinia brushed each turnover with an egg-white glaze and sprinkled a generous portion of sugar on top before placing the tray in the oven. Then she grabbed a dishtowel and began to wipe the dishes dry while she waited for the turnovers to bake.

Bethany stopped scrubbing and turned thoughtfully toward Levinia. "Do you suppose enough time has passed that *Daed* would let me open up that bakery?"

Levinia gasped. "I don't want to be around when you bring up *that* subject. He will probably yell, or he might just ignore you and pretend he didn't hear you—he likes to do that a lot. But I can guarantee he will not permit it."

Bethany went back to the chore of scraping the skillet used to scramble the eggs. "I'm going to ask him anyway, and I'm not taking no for an answer!"

The kitchen filled with the warm aroma of cinnamon and apples. Levinia breathed in, satisfied with the treat they would share with Nate's cousin, Adam, and his *familye*. They'd been distant neighbors forever, and Levinia had even entertained

Frau Troyer for several quilting and canning bees, but now that she was involved with Nate, she hoped to impress her future *familye.*

"*Ach,* I don't know how you can be defiant toward *Daed* and get away without a sound lashing behind the barn."

Bethany rinsed the skillet and placed it on the towel on the counter for Levinia to dry, and then went about finishing the last of the cooking utensils.

"I know you think *Daed* is tough, but you need to know that he no longer has the strength *or* the will to enforce the rules he tries to lay down."

Levinia looked at her sister curiously. "I think you are just a little on the side of being naïve where *Daed* is concerned, because he is certainly tough, and he *will* enforce the rules when pushed far enough. I, for one, do not want to push him to see just how far he can be pushed. But it seems you do, so let me know when you decide you are going to carry through with your *narrish* little plan, and I'll be certain I'm miles away from here."

Bethany giggled. "You are a chicken!"

Levinia scoffed. "When it comes to *Daed,* I suppose I will always be *afraid* of him, but now that I have Nate, I will have *him* to step up in front of me and protect me."

Bethany laughed heartily. "You better hope he doesn't have to do any defending before those ribs of his heal."

"I have a feeling he would brave *Daed's* temper even with several broken bones!"

Bethany sighed. "You're lucky to have him. I have to admit, I was a little jealous."

Levinia put a hand on Bethany's shoulder.

"Don't be jealous of me. Be happy for me."

"*Ach,* don't worry. It's isn't real jealousy. It's more of a sadness and loneliness."

"Well don't be sad either, little *schweschder,* because the right *mann* will come along for you, too."

"I wish I had your confidence."

Levinia picked up the pair of crocheted potholders and opened the oven, letting the cinnamon-apple turnovers scent the kitchen with mouth-watering anticipation.

"It's funny that I always thought you had complete confidence in yourself, Bethany."

Bethany shook her head. "What you think you see is really a defense and an illusion. I *act* confident to make it *appear* that I am."

Levinia chuckled. "I suppose I never thought about that. It's a pretty deceiving act you put on. Unfortunately, I don't even have enough confidence to *act* confident."

Bethany let out the stopper at the bottom of the sink and swished the suds down the drain. "I think we are getting way off-track with this conversation. I'm going to put on a dry apron while those heavenly smelling turnovers cool so I can get them over to your would-be *familye.*"

Levinia's heart quickened its pace at the thought of it. Though she'd talked to Adam and his *mamm* plenty of times, she was suddenly nervous about the impending meeting. It would be as if she was meeting them all over again. The circumstances were different now. Suddenly she'd gone from being simply a neighbor to being *familye.*

She readied a tray of the leftover meal she'd been keeping warm in the lower part of oven to take it to Nate. Giddiness overtook her as she lovingly prepared everything just right. She'd been a servant all her life to her *daed,* but to serve Nate was a joy because he loved her, and her heart overflowed with love for him too.

CHAPTER 13

"Bethany, what's wrong?"

Levinia felt dread traveling through her veins, churning up emotion like a waterspout over Willow Creek.

Bethany narrowed her gaze on Nate as she took her sister gently by the hand and guided her toward the small kitchen of the loft. Before they could exit the bedroom where Levinia had been enjoying a leisurely breakfast with Nate, her path collided with a very beautiful young Amish woman.

Levinia gazed into the woman's sea-glass, blue eyes and trailed over her shiny, flaxen hair. Her skin was flawless, like the porcelain dolls that are sold at the gift shop in town. Her slender hands rested on perfectly trim hips as her gaze stretched around Levinia.

Tall, lanky and plain, Levinia.

"Nate! I've been so worried about you!"

Nate's gaze darted between Levinia and the young woman, shock rendering him momentarily speechless.

Please, Lord, Levinia begged silently. *Don't let her be who I think she is.*

"Miriam, what are you doing here?"

"I went by and had *kaffi* with your *schweschder,* and she told me her husband is tending the animals for you through the remainder of the harvest because you plan to stay here. Why did you leave without telling me *goodbye?*"

"You shouldn't have come here, Miriam."

Nate looked past Levinia at Miriam, who had brushed by her and was fast-approaching his bedside.

"Why wouldn't I come to you, my love?"

Her words dripped with honey, but her tone was soaked with vinegar. She pounced on the mattress beside him, startling Levinia with her boldness. Nate, however, didn't seem surprised by her actions and ignored her.

Nate still had not looked at Levinia, but she had heard enough. She wasn't going to stick around long enough for him to publicly humiliate her. The embarrassment she felt at having Bethany witness this was more than she could bear. She ran from the room, unable to handle the sight of *Miriam* sitting so close to the man she loved.

Nate called after her, but she was compelled to leave the loft.

She couldn't breathe.

Tears choked her almost to the point of suffocation. A myriad of emotions ripped through her, each twisting at her heart, wringing it out like the laundry on washday. Every breath she pulled in became more strenuous than the last as she struggled to make sense of her *relationship* with Nate.

Her feet prodded down the steps of the loft, propelling her into an automated state of mind, though her thoughts remained very much with Nate and the woman he *really* loved.

Had they had a squabble and he'd decided to put some distance between them? Or was the reality of it more grueling than Levinia dared to imagine? She didn't want to think that she'd kissed another woman's betrothed, let alone that she'd fallen in love with him. She began to second-guess herself, wondering if her feelings for Nate had been nothing more than the makings of a *first crush.*

"Levinia, wait," Bethany called after her.

Waiting wasn't a problem for Levinia; moving was. Her feet felt planted in the earth like the tall stalks of corn growing in their field, only she didn't feel as graceful. Still, she wanted to bolt instead of facing Bethany.

"I think you should know that I told Adam to pack up Nate and take him back to his farm. He should be here soon with the buggy. I suspected as much about this Miriam Schrock. I'm so sorry Levinia, but it's better you find out now, than to take up with a liar and a cheater like Nate."

Levinia's breath caught in her throat as she stifled a sob. She would not cry over this man.

The hinges of the screen door squeaked the presence of Miriam. Levinia looked up at the graceful beauty as she trailed pretentiously down the stairs toward them. Levinia's first instinct was to run, but her legs still felt wobbly. Besides, it was best to get this over with and put her silly notions of a future with Nate behind her so she could go back to her life.

Ach, what life?

"I suppose I should thank you for *helping* my Nate," Miriam began in a condescending tone. "But I think it's best you know of my involvement with him in order avoid any more *confusion* on your part.

I can certainly understand you developing a *crush* on the *mann. Ach,* surely you must know he was only being kind to you because you were helping him. You can't possibly believe he would prefer *you* over me. You live so simple here it's obvious you take Plain living to an extreme. After all, if you weren't wearing a dress, I'd have wondered if you were a *mann!*"

Levinia's mind went numb and she tuned out the hurtful words. She couldn't hear any more of it lest she crumble inwardly like a dilapidated barn. If she didn't feel so numb inside, she'd have run to the next county before stopping, but her legs just wouldn't take her away no matter how badly she wanted them to.

Bethany pulled on Levinia's arm, but she couldn't budge her from the spot she'd not yet moved from. "Let's go, Levinia. We don't have to stand here and be insulted by someone from another community. She thinks she's better than we are, but being from a different community and wearing fancy, colorful dresses doesn't make her any less Amish than we are."

If Levinia would have been thinking a little more clearly, she'd have sworn she'd seen Bethany stick her tongue out at Miriam.

Miriam tipped her head to the side, swinging the loose flaxen hair from her *kapp*. *"Ach,* I'm not Amish at all. Turns out, I'm adopted! I'm an *Englischer*. And *that* makes me better than *both* of you."

Levinia looked a little closer at Miriam's *perfect* skin, noting that she was wearing makeup. And though her dress might be acceptable for some other community, it seemed too fancy even for some of the rebellious Mennonite girls. Miriam was young, most likely Bethany's age, so it made sense for her to dress the way she was and to wear makeup, being that she was at the end of her *rumspringa.*

Bethany posted both her hands on her hips defensively. "We don't care what you *say* you are, but we know what we *think* you are! Your life is of no concern to us, so leave our farm and don't come back."

Levinia looked at her little sister as if she'd suddenly become someone she didn't know. She knew Bethany was free-spirited, but she'd never heard her *fight* with anyone. Normally, Levinia would reprimand her for such behavior, but right now, she wanted Miriam to leave more than Bethany did.

"It doesn't matter what you think," Miriam said, flouncing her pale, yellow frock. "Nate wants to be an *Englischer* and that is what we have in common. *You* have nothing in common with him."

The snarly look Miriam sent Levinia momentarily empowered her to harness the courage to fight this battle herself. Her lips parted, but the words stuck there like the bugs hanging from the strips of flypaper suspended from the rafters of the barn. Why couldn't she be as bold as Bethany?

"As soon as Nate agrees to leave the Amish, we will become *Englischers* together and he will forget all about the mistake he made in thinking he might want to stay here and court *you*. After all, why would he want someone like you when he can have me?"

The squeak of the screen door startled Levinia out of the stupor in which Miriam's words had momentarily trapped her. Her gaze impulsively lifted to meet Nate's. Her heart involuntarily filled with pain the moment their eyes met.

"That's enough lies, Miriam," Nate called down to her.

Miriam pursed her lips and narrowed her eyes as if she was prepared to charge at Nate like a penned-up bull ready to fight. She looked up at him with a piercing glare in her eyes. "Perhaps you should take your own advice. You obviously didn't tell this poor *Tomboy* that you declared love for me the night of your *schweschder's* wedding."

"I did no such thing! You followed me around the whole night and wouldn't leave me alone."

Levinia watched Nate grab the banister with determination, wincing with every step he took down the staircase toward them. For a moment, she was tempted to go to Nate and help him, but Miriam's words reminded her that he wasn't hers.

Behind her, the clip-clop of horse's hooves and the grinding of buggy wheels against the gravel driveway brought her back to reality.

Adam hopped out of the buggy without setting the brake and sprinted up the stairs to help his cousin down the rest of them. "I'm sorry about not getting here sooner, but I had to drop off *mei schweschder,* Libby, in town. I tried to stop Miriam from coming here, but she wouldn't listen to me."

Nate paused his journey down the steps long enough to glare at Miriam. "She doesn't listen to anyone. In fact, she doesn't even listen to reason."

Miriam planted her dainty hands on her dainty hips angrily. "You are the one who doesn't listen. If you did, you wouldn't have left without me. I'm the only one who understands how much you want to leave the community—we are meant to be together."

Nate chuckled. "I only left to get away from *you!*"

Miriam gritted her teeth. "You left because you're a coward who goes back on promises."

"I never promised you anything," Nate retorted.

"Having your way with me was an unspoken promise—a commitment to…"

Nate took an aggressive step toward her. "I never did anything except kiss you—once, and I wish I hadn't because when I realized what a shallow, self-absorbed person you were, I wanted nothing to do with you!"

Miriam pushed out her lower lip. "But I thought you wanted to live among the *Englisch* with me."

"You misunderstood me when I said I wanted to see what being an *Englischer* was all about, just as you misunderstood the kiss between us. When you showed up at *mei schweschder's* wedding, I told you I wasn't in love with you. I wish I'd never stopped to help you that day when your horse threw a shoe, and I wish I'd never impulsively kissed you that day either. You haven't left me alone since, and I don't understand why you can't get that I don't love you! I don't intend to have a future with you outside *or* inside of the community. You misunderstood my kindness for something else."

Miriam stamped her foot and let out an angry cry. "I didn't misunderstand anything. You should do the honorable thing and marry me."

Nate blew out a discouraging breath. "I'm not going to marry you over one kiss and a conversation about leaving the community."

Miriam leered at him. "*Ach,* it was much more than a simple kiss and we *both* know it."

CHAPTER 14

"Adam, fetch the Bishop. Bring him here so he can settle this once and for all," Nate demanded.

Miriam folded her arms across her ample bosom and pursed her lips. "Yes, Adam, fetch the Bishop."

Adam turned toward his buggy, but Bethany caught him by the arm. "Wait a minute. No one is bringing the Bishop here. Levinia and I will have no part in the disagreement between the two of you. Go back to your farm Adam, and take these two with you."

She pointed disgustedly to Nate and Miriam while pulling on her sister's arm. "Let's get to our chores before *Daed* gets back from town. All of you need to be gone in the next few minutes."

They turned to leave, but Nate called after her.

"Levinia, wait. Don't let Miriam's lies turn you away from me. I love you!"

Levinia whipped her head around to face Nate, and Miriam stepped between them.

"You *love* her?!"

"*Jah,* I do," Nate said without taking his eyes off Levinia. "And I want us to spend every night together just the way we did last night."

"You spent the night with *her?*" Miriam shrieked.

Nate blew out a heavy sigh. "*Jah,* I did. It was the most *wunderbaar* night of *mei* whole life."

Letting out a low-pitched growl, Miriam's eyes filled with tears. "So you would take advantage of *two* women in the same week?"

"How dare you talk of *mei schweschder* that way!" Bethany screamed at her. "Get off our farm before I throw you off myself."

Levinia glared at Bethany. As much as she wanted Miriam to leave, she would not tolerate violence or even the threat of violence.

Miriam ignored Bethany's threat and turned her attention back to Nate. "You made me believe you loved me!"

Nate shook his head "I don't understand how you can get all that from one kiss. I never took advantage of you."

By this time Miriam was in a full-swing bout of fake crying. Levinia recognized it since she'd heard Bethany do the same thing so many times.

"So you admit to taking advantage of *her*, but deny your involvement with me! Why would you choose a woman who is so plain and boyish compared to me?"

Nate looked at her and scoffed. "There is no comparison. The beauty Levinia has in her heart makes her the most beautiful woman in the world to me. *You,* on the other hand, are shallow and spoiled and self-centered. Not to mention how mean you are to others for no reason. I could never marry a woman who is so unkind to others when they have been nothing but kind to you."

"No one is ever nice to me!" Miriam complained.

Bethany stepped forward, kicking up a little dirt onto Miriam's pristine, white, canvas shoes. "Perhaps it's because you are just not a likeable person. You haven't been here more than ten minutes, and everyone here seems to be of the general mind to dislike you!"

"I don't care what you say. I'm not leaving until I get a chance to talk to your Bishop," Miriam insisted.

Bethany threw her hands up in disgust. "Adam, go fetch the Bishop. Let *him* tell her what a fool she's making of herself."

She turned to Levinia and whispered in her ear.

"When Daed gets home, we are in for a sound lashing. You might be banned for your involvement with Nate. Miriam will surely tell even if you don't confess it yourself."

"But I haven't done anything wrong," Levinia whispered back. *"I don't have anything to confess."*

"Ach, we both know it doesn't matter that you're innocent, Miriam will obviously lie and say anything she has to in order to make you look like you're in the wrong instead of her being the one at fault for wrong-doing. People like Miriam don't care about the truth because only the lies can be used as weapons, and they thrive on hurting others."

Bethany pulled her into the house while Adam went down the road to fetch the Bishop. They had chores they needed to get to, and if their *daed* returned in the midst of the chaos, they'd be in trouble for a lot more than the scene taking place in the yard. He was a very particular *mann* about how his *haus* was kept. In fact, he was very particular about everything, and they knew he would make the situation with Nate and Miriam *his* business— especially if it involved his daughters.

Once inside the kitchen, Levinia looked out the window at Nate, who was leaning on the banister of the stairs while Miriam flailed her arms. She could hear the woman screaming at him from inside the *haus,* but Nate ignored her. Levinia said a silent prayer that the Bishop would be able to get Miriam to tell the truth—that is, *if* she was lying about her involvement with Nate. Levinia didn't want to think that he could be capable of taking advantage of the girl. Miriam *was* beautiful, but as soon as she opened her mouth, she became as ugly as Nate described.

Was it possible that he could look past her physical beauty and not find her attractive in the least?

Levinia could see the ugliness, but she doubted a man would have an easy time looking past the obvious physical beauty. She wanted so much to believe Nate's explanation, but she didn't understand why a woman as beautiful as Miriam would lie about such a thing. It would seem she could have any man she desired, so why waste her time with one who claimed he didn't love her? Perhaps she was simply *narrish,* and there was *no* other explanation for her one-sided fixation on Nate.

Bethany nudged Levinia. "So do you believe him?"

It was a fair question, and certainly one that deserved an answer, but Levinia wasn't ready to give her opinion just yet. She studied Nate's body language as Miriam continued to berate him.

He leaned his head against the railing and remained seated on the landing, eyes closed, his left hand pressed against his ribs. She knew he wasn't in as much pain as he was pretending to be, which meant he was ignoring Miriam and acting hurt probably hoping she would leave him alone.

She continued to watch, wondering how long it would take for Miriam to stop her rant. When Nate continued to remain quiet, her words became fewer until she finally gave up. He'd ended the argument simply by not giving her anymore to argue with him about. That is certainly the same way she would have handled Miriam. She knew that sometimes the best way to defuse an angry person was to remain quiet. It always worked with her *daed,* something Bethany had not yet learned.

Watching the way Nate handled the out-of-control Miriam, she realized that he *was* telling the truth. Already she knew his gentle spirit, and knowing that about him, he could *never* love such a mean-spirited woman as Miriam. Why couldn't Miriam see that? Was her anger blocking her from seeing that he wanted nothing to do with her? Levinia could see it; anyone watching the two of them could plainly see he loathed her and regretted any involvement with her.

"*Jah,* I believe him," Levinia finally said.

CHAPTER 15

Adam returned with the Bishop, but he didn't get out of the buggy. Instead, Adam hopped out and helped Nate into the back, while instructing Miriam to Join the Bishop up front. Nate paused at the back of the buggy to look toward the main *haus* as if to bid Levinia *goodbye*.

The quietness of the kitchen made Levinia shiver as she stared out into the empty yard where Nate had been only a few moments ago. Now, it was as if he'd never even been there. A deep sadness filled her, making her wonder if she would ever recover. She'd experienced nothing but loss in her life, and this was just too much for her.

Levinia wiped her tears as she watched her father pull his buggy into the yard, his usual, anger-filled expression seemingly worse. Her heart filled with much trepidation at the possibility her father had run into Adam's buggy on the way up from the main road. Was it possible he'd spoken to the Bishop? He turned and looked toward the *haus*.

He knew.

Scurrying from the kitchen, Levinia ran up the stairs to warn Bethany, who was gathering up the throw-rugs. Levinia picked up an end of the large, braided rug in the hall and whispered in case her father had come into the *haus*.

"*Daed* just pulled up in the yard, and looks angry."

"He always looks angry," Bethany sighed. "But you don't suppose he knows, do you?"

Levinia shook her head. "I think he had just enough time to talk to the Bishop at the end of the road. They had to have run into each other. The timing is too close."

Bethany dropped the rug. "Then he knows about Nate staying in the loft."

Dropping her end of the rug, Levinia crumbled to the floor. "I don't want to face *Daed*. I don't want to have to explain to him how foolish I was to give my heart to a *mann* who is about to be forced to marry another woman."

Bethany crouched down beside her and put her arm around her shoulder. "No one said you have to tell him all of that! All we have to tell him is that we found him injured and we helped him. That's all. Nothing else."

"It's not that easy with *Daed,* and you know it. He's going to ask so many questions, you're going to think you're back in school taking a test in front of the whole class!"

Bethany leaned her elbow on her knee and rested her chin on her hand. She blew out a long, discouraging sigh.

"Stop that! I'm nervous enough without having *you* falling apart on me. You're the strong one—the one with enough guts to stand up to *Daed!*"

"*Ach,* I'm not so sure I can help you with this one," Bethany said quietly. "You might be on your own."

Levinia narrowed her gaze at Bethany. "I didn't do *any* of this by myself! You were right there with me carrying Nate up from the creek and into the loft."

Bethany stood up and put her fists on her hips.

"It didn't take you long to use *that* against me, did it? If I didn't know any better, I'd say you tricked me into helping you so you didn't have to be the only one to blame for all of this."

Levinia lowered her head in shame. "The thought did cross *mei* mind. But I'm sorry!"

Before she could answer, they heard creaking on the stairs. They looked at each other wide-eyed.

"*Help!*" Levinia mouthed to Bethany.

Bethany rolled her eyes, and Levinia knew she was on her own. She took a deep breath and braced herself for the worst conversation she was about to have with her father since Daniel's funeral.

"Bethany, go out to the barn and tend to *mei* horse. She had a long trip into town and back, and needs a *gut* rubdown."

Levinia swallowed the lump in her throat, but kept her eyes to the floor. He was sending Bethany out of the *haus*—out of earshot.

This was not a good sign.

He was going to raise his voice for sure and for certain, and she was trapped between him and the stairwell. There would be no backing away from him should he decide to strike her. She prayed he would think her to be too old to administer a sound lashing.

"I ran into the Bishop on the way up to the *haus* just now. He tells me you helped a young *mann* from an Ohio community," he began in his usual, stern monotone. "It's my understanding that he stayed in the loft above the barn."

"*Jah,*" Levinia answered without lifting her head. "He was hurt and unconscious so Bethany and I brought him here to recover."

"You brought a *mann* into this *haus*—into your *bruder's* loft without my knowledge. What if he was not Amish? He could have been dangerous, and I would not have known you were in danger."

"He told me he was Amish."

"When I saw him, he was dressed as an *Englischer*, and the young woman he was with was dressed the same."

"He's not *with* her. She chased him here, but he doesn't want to marry her!"

"Silence, *dochder,*" his voice rumbled. "The Bishop stepped outside Adam's buggy and approached me so he could talk freely. The two *Englischers* are to be married if they intend to stay in the community."

"But he's not going to..." Levinia started to argue, but thought it best to keep her thoughts to herself regarding Nate.

"Don't make me think you have an interest in that rebel, *dochder.*"

"*Nee.*"

"As for the disrespect of your *bruder's* memory; I will not tolerate you spending any time in that loft. It was for Daniel, and he will never be able to use it because..."

"Because I let him die? Is that what you were going to say?"

"Don't be disrespectful to me, *dochder.*"

"*Ach, mei* name is Levinia! You haven't spoken *mei* name since Daniel's funeral when you blamed me for his death."

"You should have gone down the road to get the doctor. You took the coward's way out and called for an *Englisch* ambulance. It would have taken less time to get the doctor here than to wait for that ambulance."

Levinia felt a thick sob catch in her throat. "I was afraid to leave him that long—there was too much blood."

"You should have done the right thing. Daniel would have wanted you to do the right thing."

Levinia plucked an angry tear from her cheek.

"Daniel wanted me to have a happy life. Right before he died, he made me promise I would stop wasting *mei* life being a *mamm* to Bethany and a servant to you! He wanted me to get a husband and be loved for once in *mei* life instead of being wanted only as a servant and *mamm* to your *other dochder.*"

"He was *mei* only son, and *you* let him die!"

Levinia broke into uncontrollable sobs. "I didn't let him die! He was the one who told me to call the ambulance."

His red-rimmed eyes glared at her. "*Mei* son would not have asked for such a foolish thing. It was *your* poor judgment that brought him to his end. He was a *gut buwe,* and he won't be able to carry on the *familye* name because you acted selfishly and put your own needs before his."

"I won't continue to rival Daniel for your attention *Daed,"* she said as calmly as possible. "Daniel is gone. He's with *Mamm* in Heaven and he isn't coming back. But I'm here and I can't live with your resentment any longer. Even if I don't marry, I think it's time for me to move on. I'll be packing *mei* things and moving to the B&B. I've been offered a job that comes with room and board. I didn't accept because of *mei* obligations here, but I can no longer stay where I'm not wanted."

She walked past him and he didn't say anything to stop her.

CHAPTER 16

Levinia silently packed her small suitcase, tears running down her cheeks, a large accumulation of tears hanging precariously from the end of her nose and ready to drip onto her folded clothes.

Her father hadn't said a word to her when she'd told him she was leaving.

He hadn't tried to stop her.

He had been unyielding for too long.

It was obvious he no longer cared what she did, and at this point, Levinia didn't either. Hurt and anger would drive her to prove to him she was worth more than her dead brother. More than being a servant and mother to her sister. More than a naïve pushover, and certainly better-suited for Nate than Miriam.

She wondered what was missing from *Miriam's* life that had made *her* so bitter. Was it worth even *trying* to figure out what drove Miriam? Funny, but it would seem they both had two things in common; neither of them had a mother—and they both loved the same man.

Albeit, Miriam's *love* for Nate was one-sided and very misguided, but in her own way, she seemed convinced her *love* for him was genuine. If Levinia didn't know any better, she'd think Miriam's love was misdirected—almost like an attachment to fill a void in her life. Mourning the loss of a first love, perhaps, or even the loss of her unknown birth-mother. Whatever it was, it would seem as if the void in Miriam's life had caused her to have an unhealthy attachment to Nate.

It didn't matter what Levinia thought. Miriam's life was her own. If only Levinia could find a way to keep Miriam from taking out her unhappiness onto her and using that to try to destroy Levinia's chance for a future with Nate. Levinia truly loved Nate—unconditionally.

Sadly, it would seem Miriam had not learned to love that way. Her love was self-seeking and very conditional. Levinia hadn't missed Miriam's change in attitude as soon as Nate rejected her. Suddenly, it seemed, she felt Nate *owed* her something— something she was *not* entitled to. And for that, she would punish him by forcing him to marry her.

Bethany poked her head in the bedroom door and scowled as she eyed the open suitcase spread across the bed. "What are you doing? You can't leave me here with *Daed!*"

"*Ach,* you don't need me anymore. No one needs me. No one *wants* me!"

Levinia released a strangled sob.

Bethany crossed the room slowly, offering her sister comfort with a limp embrace. "I'm certain he loves you."

Levinia knew her sister was referring to Nate and not her father. Normally, it would have been a comforting thought, but she feared it was too late to matter whether he loved her or not. Their love for each other would not be enough to prevent Miriam from working her best lies to keep them apart. But did she really have that power? As long as neither of them stood up to her, Miriam held all the control. Levinia knew she wasn't strong enough to stand up against a woman as mean-spirited as Miriam, and Nate seemed to believe that keeping quiet would solve everything.

Did Levinia have enough faith to wait this out and hope that *Gott* would intervene? It would seem she had no other choice.

"Have faith," Bethany said as if she could read Levinia's thoughts. "You and Nate were brought together by *Gott,* and He will not let you be torn apart simply because this woman chooses to tell her lies to everyone who will listen. Sooner or later she will be found out for the spiteful, jealous liar she is, and then the Bishop will run her out of this community, and we will be rid of her for sure and for certain!"

"*Denki,* little *schweschder.*"

"*Ach,* it's the least I can do after I left you to be ambushed by *Daed.* I'm sorry about that. I heard what you said to him about Daniel. You're not the only one competing against our deceased *bruder* for *Daed's* attention."

"*Ach,* little *schweschder,* I had no idea you felt the same way."

Bethany reached into Levinia's suitcase and fingered the material of a blue dress she'd never seen before.

"What is this?"

Levinia sighed. "I made this dress after Daniel died. I'd promised him I would marry someday, and sewing this dress helped me to mourn for him—as a way of keeping that promise. I had no idea I would ever really get married, and I certainly never thought I would meet someone as *wunderbaar* as Nate. But now—well unless *Gott* fixes this, I won't have any use for this dress."

"Then why do you have it packed?"

Levinia giggled. "Just in case! Besides, if we are never coming back here, I don't want to leave it here because it reminds me of Daniel."

Bethany pulled her dresses off the pegs on the far wall of the bedroom they shared and stuffed them into Levinia's suitcase without saying a word. There were four other bedrooms in the *haus,* but they had always preferred to share. It was the largest bedroom in the old farmhouse, and they had shared it since Bethany's second birthday. Her crib still sat in the corner of the room where their mother had placed it all those years ago.

To this day, Levinia kept it dusted and the linens would get washed every few months to keep them fresh. There had never been a reason to move it. Their mother had put it there, and they had been content to leave it as a remembrance of her.

Now, it seemed, they would be leaving the crib and their mother behind, once and for all. It was too late to change their minds. They would leave their father and his bitterness behind them and start a new life.

CHAPTER 17

"Do you suppose Bess will take me in, too?"

"*Jah,* but together we will have to work for one salary."

Levinia smoothed stray blond hairs from Bethany's cheek before she rang the bell at the front desk in the lobby of the B&B. The wide hallway of the one-hundred-year-old home boasted a wooden staircase that opened up to the floor above, and several sets of French doors opening to the parlor and formal living and dining rooms. The hardwood floors were worn with age, but still very shiny, and the area rugs were all freshly swept clean. Wood panels, thick with several years of paint, decorated the lower portion of the walls, and curved around the corner wall that led to a private room. It was the only main-level bedroom, and it was set aside as the proprietor's private quarters. This was indeed a grand old *haus* with a welcoming porch that stretched the length of the home and wrapped around on both ends. Levinia could feel at home here, couldn't she?

"Why do we have to share a salary?" Bethany asked, interrupting Levinia's reverie.

"She only needs *one* employee to cook and clean the rooms."

Bethany took a look around at the expanse of the entry-hall. "For this place? This place has eleven bedrooms and more bathrooms than that! It's the biggest *haus* in this county. It would take a staff of at least seven to run this place properly."

"Bess and Jessup do a lot of the work, and Silvia works hard for this place. Her *schweschder,* Susie will be staying on and working with us if Bess gives us the job, so don't worry about how much work there will be. Whatever it is, we will do it together."

"But for *one* salary?"

"I will do the cooking and you can serve, but we will do the cleaning together. I'm certain she won't object to us sharing a room."

It was too late to turn back now. They stood in the lobby, suitcase in hand, prepared to work and live away from their father once and for all. Levinia was determined not to let her father or Nate be the downfall of her state of happiness. She would have faith that her life would work out according to *Gott's* plan.

Bess strolled in though the swinging door of the kitchen, towel-drying her hands. She was getting on in years, and her hard work was beginning to show in the deep creases of her forehead that glistened with perspiration. She let her gaze fall to the suitcase in Levinia's hand and looked at her curiously. "I thought you said you couldn't take the job? But even so, you remember it doesn't start until next month when Silvia gets married."

Levinia swallowed down the lump forming quickly in her throat. She didn't want Bess to know her business with her *daed,* but she'd neglected to rehearse what reason she would give the older woman for why she was accepting the job. She *had* forgotten the job didn't start for another month. She didn't have the means to pay room-and-board for two for an entire month before the job opened up.

"Perhaps...I made a hasty...decision in coming here," Levinia stuttered.

She turned to leave, but Bethany caught her by the arm. "We will be needing a room then."

Bess paused to study the two girls standing before her. It was obvious to her they were in need for some reason or another, and it was evident they had no intention of sharing that information just yet. But needy they were, and being neighbors, she would help them as long as she could.

"Since Silvia seems busy lately with wedding plans, it seems I'm spending more time in the kitchen than I want to in order to pick up the slack. If you two can fill in for me, I'll give you a room in exchange for your help. But *only* on the condition that I don't have a reservation for the room. If I get full-up, you'll have to start paying for the room to hold it from a paying customer."

"*Nee,*" Levinia began.

"We'll take it," Bethany interrupted her.

Bess pulled a key-ring out of the desk drawer and reluctantly handed it to Bethany while Levinia stood there in shock. "Are you sure this is what you want to do, Levinia?"

She nodded automatically and took the key.

CHAPTER 18

Nate winced every time Adam's buggy hit a rut in the country road between his cousin's farm and Levinia's. The sun was barely up, and the birds hadn't even begun their morning rituals yet, but Nate knew Levinia would be up working hard the way she did.

Though he was still in a lot of pain, Nate was eager to see her and just didn't want to wait another minute. After the way he'd left things with her the day before when Miriam had made her scene, he felt he had to give her an explanation. He knew he'd be lucky if Levinia agreed to listen to him, especially given the grave news he had to share with her. Unfortunately, he felt he owed her the truth of his possible fate before she heard it from someone else—namely, Miriam.

His introduction to the community Bishop had been grueling, to say the least. After hearing Miriam's *confession,* the Bishop had informed him if the girl's story didn't clear him, he'd be forced to marry her or be shunned. He'd taken the classes for baptism already, and had agreed to take the baptism tomorrow, and then the wedding would take place right after. The *only* reason Nate agreed to take the baptism was because he hoped it would afford him the opportunity to marry Levinia. He had *no* intention on marrying Miriam, even if meant he would be shunned. But Levinia didn't know that yet, so he hoped she would give him the chance to explain.

"Are you sure you want to do this?" Adam asked him.

"*Jah,* I'm sure."

"Sounds like you have doubts. If you do, let me know before we pull into her driveway. Her *daed* is not the easiest person to get along with."

Nate chuckled. "I met him yesterday, remember? But I'm not going to see her *daed*—this time!"

Adam slowed his horse before turning into Levinia's driveway. "You really think you're going to get out of this with Miriam so you can marry Levinia?"

Nate nodded confidently. "I have faith that the truth will set me free."

Adam turned the horse into the driveway, but let him stroll down the lane, hoping the gentle clip-clop of his hooves would not alert Levinia's father of their visit. They managed to reach the house, without being seen by anyone, but it looked as though no one was even home. With Adam's assistance, Nate slipped from the buggy and went to the kitchen door.

He knocked three times, but there was no answer. He turned around to get advice from his cousin, when Levinia's father came toward him from the barn.

"She isn't here," her father said gruffly.

Wearing his Amish attire this time, Nate tipped his hat politely. "When do you expect her return?"

The man walked past without looking up.

"Don't know where she is," he said over his shoulder. "*Mei dochders* both packed their things yesterday and left home. I don't know where they are and I don't expect them back. I suppose you've put ideas in their heads about living among the *Englisch.* You had *no* right to come here and upset *mei familye* life the way you did. Go back to your own community and leave me alone. You've done enough damage here."

Nate turned around to face him. "If you're *dochders* left home, it might be because *you* have made them think you don't love them anymore, and

Levinia believes you blame her for her *bruder's* death. You need to forgive her—for her sake *and* yours."

Adam assisted Nate back into the buggy and then climbed in beside him. They looked one last time at Levinia's father to give some sort of answer, but he just stared at them.

"Just so you know," Nate said. "I love Levinia and would like to marry her. I have no intention of marrying that liar, Miriam!"

The man ignored them and walked in through the kitchen door and closed it behind him.

"That is one bitter *mann,*" Adam said as he clicked to the horse to set the buggy in the direction of home.

A deep concern set in Nate's thoughts. Where could they have gone?

ॐ∂∞

Levinia dressed quickly after nudging Bethany to get up. Even though they'd gone to sleep too early, and had even missed out on the evening meal at the B&B, they needed to get up and start earning their keep. They should have helped to serve the guests the meal last night and helped to clean up, but they'd both been so overwhelmed from the dramatic events that took place yesterday, it's no wonder they slept for more than ten hours.

Levinia pinned her apron and once again nudged at Bethany. "Get up. If we don't start working, we're going to have to start paying for this room."

Bethany stuffed the pillow over her head. "I don't care. I have money."

Levinia snatched the pillow off her head.

"Where did you get money?"

She sat up sleepily and grabbed at the pillow, but Levinia pulled it out of her reach.

"I'm not always out running around with boys like you think. I babysit for the Anderson *kinner.*"

Levinia turned up her nose. "*Ach,* the ones that are always throwing rocks?"

"*Jah,* their poor *mamm* needs a break from them a lot since her husband is always working. Sometimes, she just likes to go get groceries by herself because they throw cans in the aisles and stuff like that. Plus I sometimes help her do the wash."

Levinia shook her head. "You do the wash at *her haus,* but you won't help me with it?"

"She has an automatic washer! You *know* how much I despise hanging clothes on the line."

Levinia rolled her eyes. "They have one here, too, so you should be right at home with no excuses to do the wash."

Bethany pulled a paper bag out from under her pillow and dumped out the cash. "But she pays me *gut!*"

Levinia dropped to the bed beside Bethany and ran her hand through the stack of bills. "This is a lot of money! What were you planning on doing with that?"

Bethany frowned as she stuffed the money back into the bag. "It's over five thousand dollars, and I was thinking about buying a car."

Levinia giggled. "I always wanted to know what it was like to drive a car, but I never had the guts to do anything about it. If you want to spend your money on a car, I think that is a fine use of it. You obviously worked hard taking care of those out-of-control *kinner*. For that alone, you deserve something nice."

They both laughed. It was freeing to be able to laugh and share such things without having to look over their shoulder to be certain they were not overheard by their father—or worse yet—disturbing him in any way.

Bethany dragged herself from the bed and pulled her brown dress from the small closet in the corner of the room.

Fastening her *kapp*, Levinia sighed as she looked in the mirror. She wished she could see herself the way Nate had claimed to see her. But none of that mattered anymore. This was her life now unless a miracle brought Nate back to her.

"I'll meet you downstairs in the kitchen," she said over her shoulder to Bethany. "Hurry!"

Bethany pulled her apron over her head. "I'll be there right behind you."

Levinia closed the door and went down the service stairs to the kitchen. Silvia had already gathered the eggs and Jessup walked in just then with the morning milking, and exited without so much as a nod. For as primitive as they presented, they did use some modern conveniences that Levinia noted. She'd never had an occasion to be in the kitchen before, and she was happy to see they had a large, industrial sink for washing dishes. They also had a nine-burner gas stove and a large refrigerator and freezer. She assumed they would have to in order to keep up with health codes, but

Levinia knew it would make things easier when it came to getting Bethany to do her fair share of the workload.

"Bethany will be down in just a few minutes," Levinia said. "Where would you like me to start?"

Silvia looked up from kneading dough on the large, stainless steel island in the center of the kitchen.

"We don't usually start cooking until seven because guests like to sleep in a little. We have four guests—no, five. We just got in a young woman last night. She showed up in time to join us for the evening meal. A real pretty young woman from Ohio. She's getting married tomorrow—here. Bess agreed to hold the wedding at the last minute, so we have a lot of work to do to prepare for this wedding. We've never done a wedding on such short notice, but she only agreed to do it since we have you and Bethany for extra help now."

Levinia's heart sank to her feet and she felt the blood draining from her face. Was it possible there was another beautiful woman in town from Ohio that was getting married tomorrow? She prayed it wasn't Miriam, because that would mean she was marrying Nate—*her* Nate.

Silvia went about her chores as if Levinia wasn't even there. Carrying a stack of plates to the dining room, she nearly ran into Bethany as she entered through the swinging door.

Bethany entered the kitchen and rushed to Levinia's side. "*Schweschder,* are you alright? You look as if you're about to pass out."

"Miriam is here!" she whispered to Bethany.

"*Ach,* are you sure?"

"*Jah,*" she said, tears filling her eyes. "And she is to be married tomorrow—to Nate."

"Do you really suppose she was able to convince the Bishop of her lies?"

"It would seem so. What am I going to do?"

Bethany handed her a napkin to wipe her face.

"We aren't going to do anything until we know for sure and for certain. And when we know, we will figure it out then."

"But *we* have to help with the preparations for her wedding because she's having it *here* and we work here now! I don't want to attend that wedding, much less be a *servant* for it. "

If we must, that is what we will do," Bethany said sternly. "For now, you need to pull yourself together so I don't have to spend *mei* car money keeping a roof over our heads."

Levinia swallowed hard the lump in her throat and wiped her face before Silvia returned and saw her in that state. Bethany was right. They had a job to do, and she would not jump to conclusions. She would trust that *Gott* would answer her prayer about Nate.

CHAPTER 19

Levinia's fingers felt stiff from plucking all the feathers from the chickens to prepare for tomorrow's wedding. Perspiration rolled from the end of her nose and she swiped at it with her shoulder. Though it was a chilly morning, the blanching pot Jessup had set up over the fire-pit in the yard was making her too warm.

Her hands were raw from the blanching pot, and the laborious task of plucking some of the younger hens that had been selected because they were covered in pinfeathers, and those were not the easiest to remove.

Gott, please help me to do this task with a merry heart—even if it is for Miriam and Nate.

It was almost eight o'clock, and the guests would be expecting breakfast to be served any minute. It would be then that Levinia would find out once and for all if Miriam was indeed the guest bride. She quickly let Jessup know she was finished blanching the first batch of chickens so he would gut them. She was grateful he'd agreed to do that task for her. It wasn't like she hadn't done it before for her own *familye,* but there would be more than thirty chickens to prepare for the wedding, and that was too much for her to handle on her own. The blanching and plucking alone would take another couple of hours. She'd already spent two hours preparing the first ten.

Brushing the loose feathers from the front of her, Levinia went in through the service door to the kitchen to wash up in preparation for serving the morning meal. She hoped Bethany had fared well with working alongside Silvia in preparing the food. Cooking was *not* her sister's strong-suit, but Levinia knew it would easier for Bethany than what *she'd* spent the morning doing. Bethany had never plucked a chicken—ever. So Levinia decided the best place for her sister would be the kitchen, knowing Silvia would have enough patience to give the instruction Bethany needed.

When Levinia finished washing up, she could hear the guests gathering in the dining room. Bethany picked up the platter of various muffins and a pitcher of milk, while Levinia hoisted a tray with three kinds of juice and several stemmed glasses, and together they took a deep breath to prepare for what they would find beyond the swinging door that led to the formal dining room.

"It's show-time," Bethany whispered just before Silvia walked in ahead of them carrying a large tray full of scrambled eggs, sausage and bacon.

Levinia struggled to balance the tray she carried when her gaze focused on Miriam sitting at one end of the large dining room table. Almost immediately, Miriam flashed a look of disgust toward Levinia, making her feel even more uncomfortable than she ever thought she could. She had nothing to be ashamed of. She was putting in an honest day's work. So why did Miriam's presence make her feel so unsure of herself?

Certainly Miriam's over-confident demeanor was part of what made up her aggressive nature. Levinia had already learned that Miriam had a way of *forcing* her way on people, and if they didn't do exactly what she wanted them to do, a punishment was sure to follow. Levinia had already unintentionally crossed paths with the woman, and Miriam's very presence shook her confidence.

Miriam pinched the end of her nose dramatically when Levinia stood near her to place the stemware and juice in front of her. "You smell like dead chickens. You're causing me to lose my appetite, and I must keep up my strength. After all, tomorrow is my wedding day, and I wouldn't want to have a bad wedding night with Nate."

Levinia blew out an angry breath as she finished placing the stemware around the table, finding it very difficult to ignore Miriam's comment about spending her wedding night with the man *she* loved. Levinia quickly exited the room, waiting until she reached the safety of the kitchen before she let out a strangled cry.

Gott, please don't let Miriam force Nate to marry her, she cried out. *I love him and I really believe you have blessed me to be his fraa. I pray that Miriam's lies will be found out in time. Help me to have faith.*

Bethany and Silvia trailed into the kitchen just then and rushed to her side.

"Why did you let her talk to you that way?"

Levinia sniffled. "Because she is a guest here, and I am nothing but a servant. This is *mei* life now. I work here, and will for probably the rest of *mei* spinster life, unless *Gott* sees fit to change this situation around."

Levinia sobbed even harder while Bethany filled Silvia in on what had happened. Pulling the end of her apron to her face to wipe it, Levinia choked a little. She did smell bad. Miriam was right about that.

"That snooty girl doesn't have the final word," Bethany said. "*Gott* does."

"Miriam can't take something away from you that *Gott* has blessed you with," Silvia offered. "Have faith that *you* will be the one to marry Nate if it be *Gott's Wille.*"

"How am I going to get through that wedding tomorrow when *mei* heart is breaking?" Levinia sobbed.

"This isn't over until the Bishop declares them as wed, so don't give up hope, dear *schweschder.*"

Levinia stood up and wiped her face, and then crossed to the back end of the kitchen and took a clean service apron from the pantry closet. "You're right. I'm not going to let her win. Her lies will *not* get between me and the man I love, no matter how many people she has listening to her lies. The truth will set Nate free from that evil woman!"

Bethany smiled. "I believe I'm starting to rub off on you a little bit, big *schweschder!"*

"Ach, I believe you're right," Levinia agreed.

She wiped her remaining tears, and all three went back out to the dining room to finish serving, presenting a united front against Miriam's trickery.

CHAPTER 20

Levinia shook as she prepared food for the wedding that was to take place in less than an hour. She hadn't slept more than twenty minutes all night, tossing and turning so much Bethany had gotten after her for not having more faith. It wasn't that she lacked faith in *Gott* to fix the situation, she lacked the confidence that the humans involved would not use their free will to create a different plan from *Gott's*.

She'd prayed for wisdom for the Bishop, and for Miriam to suddenly grow a conscience. She didn't have much faith in the latter. What she did have faith in was her love for Nate, and his love for her.

Love never fails, she kept telling herself.

As she finished working on the last of the celery casseroles, she wondered what had become of Bethany. She hadn't seen her in some time, and she'd made the excuse of putting the table cloths on all the tables at least twenty minutes ago. If her sister had run off and given up on this job already, Levinia was going to have a tough time supporting the two of them.

A high-pitched scream interrupted Levinia's reverie. It sounded like Miriam. Several screams, accompanied by stomping down the front stairwell alerted the entire house that Miriam was upset about something. Levinia exited the kitchen door to see what all the commotion was, when an angry Miriam ran into her.

She held up a dirty, blue dress and shook it in Levinia's face. "Look what your sister did to my dress! I caught her putting chicken guts on my wedding dress!"

Levinia looked beyond Miriam at Bethany who had strolled in behind Miriam, wearing an obvious look of satisfaction on her face.

"Tell her Miriam, why it is that you conveniently have that wedding dress with you! Tell *mei schweschder* how you planned this whole thing, and how you lied to force Nate to marry you."

"I will tell her no such thing! I only said that because I caught you trying to sabotage my dress. Well, naturally I went along with you because I didn't want you soiling my wedding dress," Miriam stuttered. "Now what am I supposed to get married in?"

Bethany stuck her tongue out at Miriam. "It doesn't matter because Nate isn't even going to show up. He doesn't want to marry you, he wants to marry Levinia!"

Miriam stormed off in a fitful cry. "You'll be sorry—both of you!"

When she was out of earshot, Levinia reprimanded Bethany for doing something so spiteful and childish.

"You're just a pushover," Bethany muttered.

"*Nee,* but *Gott* commands us not to repay evil with evil."

"*Jah,* you're right. Let's go finish preparing the food for her wedding so she can kick us some more."

"Honestly, Bethany, I don't know where you get your attitude from. Vengeance is for the Lord, not for us."

Bethany sighed. "I hate it when you're right."

Levinia walked into the kitchen with Bethany. She didn't want to prepare the food for Miriam's wedding any more than her sister did, but she wouldn't let her know that. She would always have the attitude of being a mother to her younger sister, and for that reason alone she would suffer through being a *gut* example to her no matter how painful it was for her.

CHAPTER 21

Levinia looked out the side window at all the benches set up in front of the gazebo. They were nearly all filled. Had the entire community come to witness this wedding? In the back, buggies filled the parking area and they were beginning to line up alongside of the long driveway leading to the *haus*.

Suddenly, her eyes focused on Nate, who was walking up the lane with Adam.

He was dressed for his wedding.

Panic filled Levinia as reality set in.

He'd shown up.

He was actually going to go through with it.

Her hand clamped across her mouth as she stifled a sob. She couldn't fall apart. It wasn't over yet. He was a *gut* and honorable *mann*. But was he so honorable that he should go through with marrying a woman simply because she'd tricked him? Most likely it was so, and the sooner she faced it the better off she would be. Like it or not, she had a job to do, and she would need to go in there and tend to the guests with a smile pasted on her face, or she might lose it.

The kitchen door opened just then and in walked her *daed*. "Hello, *dochder*—Levinia."

Levinia collapsed into the nearest chair, stunned at her father's presence. But more than that, it was the first time he'd spoken her name since Daniel's funeral.

"I know you're surprised to see me here," he began. "I wanted you to know that I don't blame you for Daniel's—for Daniel's *death.*"

He didn't look her in the eye, and she could tell he was having trouble getting the words out.

She felt sorry for him. She loved him. More than that, she felt respect for him for the first time since she was a young girl, too young to realize his selfish ways and how they'd affected her life.

"I also want you to know that I'm sorry for expecting you to take on the chore of being *mamm* to Bethany. I should have married one of the women in the community so you'd have a proper *mamm* again and wouldn't have to raise your *schweschder,* but I loved your *mamm* so much I just couldn't bring myself to marrying another."

"Ach, I understand that."

She really did understand loving someone so much that she couldn't imagine ever loving anyone else. She loved Nate that much.

"The Bishop told me what happened with the young *mann—N*ate. I'm sorry for the outcome, but I've prayed things will work out for the two of you."

He'd prayed for her?

Tears rolled down Levinia's cheeks as she slipped into her *daed's* waiting arms. "I'm sorry I left and took Bethany with me."

"I'd like you both to come home," he said in a loving tone.

He sounded different.

He sounded kind.

He sounded sincere.

"I'd like that too."

Levinia felt relief wash over her. No matter what happened today, she and Bethany had a place to go home to.

CHAPTER 22

Levinia couldn't take her eyes off Nate as she peeked out the service door. He looked so handsome. He'd asked to talk to her, but she couldn't bring herself to seeing him except from afar. She knew she'd broken his heart, but her heart was breaking just thinking of him going through with this wedding. Hadn't he been the one to say he wouldn't marry Miriam even if it meant he would be shunned?

What had happened to that declaration?

Surely if he intended not to go through with it he would have left her at the altar. Unfortunately, Nate was not that dishonorable. She prayed he only showed up to give Miriam one last chance to tell the truth.

"We have nothing left to do until it's time to serve the guests—*if* the wedding goes through, so let's go sit at the back and watch."

Levinia whipped her head around and scowled at Bethany and Silvia. "Are you *narrish?* I'm not watching that *mann* marry that woman!"

Bethany hooked her arm sternly into Levinia's and yanked her out the kitchen door into the yard. "That *mann* is the *mann* you love, and you will go watch to see if *Gott* has truly blessed you or not."

Levinia allowed Bethany to pull her along, feeling so numb at this point, she didn't know if she would burst into tears or crumble into a million pieces.

As they walked toward the back of the benches, Miriam exited the side door nearest the gazebo.

"Miriam is wearing your wedding dress, Levinia!" Bethany shouted.

Several members of the community looked toward the commotion, and Levinia froze in place. She couldn't move, she couldn't think straight.

"I warned you that you'd be sorry!" Miriam said, contempt dripping from her words. She smiled maliciously. "Now you get to watch me marry the man you love—wearing *your* wedding dress!"

Bethany took an aggressive step toward her, but Levinia and Silvia held her back.

"You are a miserable, evil person!" Bethany screamed at her.

Miriam smiled even wider. "Perhaps, but I'm about to be Mrs. Nathan Troyer!"

Miriam turned her back to them dramatically and walked to the gazebo where Nate and the

Bishop waited for her. She took her place beside Nate and faced the Bishop.

Nate turned to Levinia as she walked past the gazebo and winked at her.

Levinia clenched Bethany's arm and smiled widely. "He still loves me, and he has a plan to get himself out of this mess!"

CHAPTER 23

Levinia sat down on the bench automatically. With Bethany and Silvia on either side of her, she tried not to think and tried not to feel. She feared that if she gave in to her feelings she would break down and fall apart. If Miriam won this, as it appeared she had, then she would need to stay strong lest she lose her mind completely. She tried not to hope too much, tried not to expect too much. Even though Nate had given her the signal that he loved her, there was still the very large obstacle of

Miriam's lies that stood between them. She prayed whatever he had planned would work.

Adam and Libby sank down on the bench beside them, and Libby nudged Bethany. "I still don't understand why *mei* cousin is marrying that girl. He doesn't even like her."

Bethany and Libby had been friends since they could crawl, but they hadn't seen each other in the past two days since she and Levinia had moved into the B&B.

Bethany leaned over Libby and glared at Adam.

"You didn't tell her why Nate's marrying her?"

Adam shrugged.

"When Miriam showed up at *mei* cousin, Amanda's, wedding and got in that big fight with Nate, I knew then how much he hated her," Libby began. "She accused him of leading her on and making her think that he loved her. When he told her he wished he'd never kissed her in the first place, I thought I was going to fall on the ground laughing. She actually thought he loved her after only *one* kiss!"

"She still thinks it," Bethany said. "Except now, she's claiming Nate took advantage of her that night."

"That's not true," Libby said. "After Nate told her to leave him alone, I overhead Miriam on her cell phone talking to some guy asking him to pick her up. I followed her to the end of the road and watched her get into a car with an *Englischer*. She kissed him after she got in, and then they drove off. Miriam never came back to the wedding, and we both stayed over at Nate's *haus* that night."

Bethany grabbed Libby by the arm and yanked her to her feet. "You have to tell the Bishop this and stop the wedding!"

Adam pulled on Libby's arm and forced her back down gently beside him. "Stay here and wait."

Just then, a young man walked up to the gazebo.

"That's him!" Libby whispered. "That's the one she drove off with that night."

"*Ach,* are you sure?" Levinia asked.

"*Jah,* I'm sure. I couldn't forget that spiky blonde hair of his."

The look of shock on Miriam's face as the young man walked up to her would not soon be forgotten by Levinia. She watched in shock herself.

"R-Ray," Miriam stammered. "What are you doing here?"

The hurtful look in his eyes was disheartening.

"The real question is—what are *you* doing here?"

"I'm getting married as you can very well see," she said snottily. "How did you know I was here?"

Ray pointed to Nate. "He called me from your cell phone after you left it in his cousin's buggy. He told me how you lied and was forcing him to marry you."

"I didn't lie, and I'm not forcing him."

Ray shook his head. "I really thought you cared about *me*. You cared enough to spend the weekend with me, but not enough to marry me, obviously."

"I *never* spent the weekend with you! We're only friends."

"That's a lie," Libby shouted from the back of the community. "I saw you get in the car with him the night of Amanda's wedding. You kissed him when you got in the car, and you never came back. Nate couldn't have taken advantage of you that night because *mei bruder* and I stayed at his *haus* after the wedding."

Miriam let out a low-pitch growl.

The Bishop then turned to Miriam. "If you intend to remain in the community, you must confess your transgressions."

She growled at Nate. "I have nothing to confess. I'm better than this. I'm an *Englischer!* I don't care if I stay in the community. You're all backward and primitive." She turned back to Nate. "I want my cell phone back. You had *no* right to go through it."

"I had *every* right. Your lies could have kept me from marrying the woman I love—Levinia."

Miriam growled at Nate again, and then turned to Ray. "Let's go!" she demanded.

"I don't want to go anywhere with you! You're nothing but a liar." He stormed off toward his car, leaving Miriam dumbfounded.

The Bishop came forward and addressed Miriam. "If you will not confess, you must leave."

Miriam stormed into the B&B muttering under her breath that she would rather die than to give a confession just to stay in the community.

After a moment of shocking silence, the Bishop asked Levinia to come up to the gazebo and take her place next to Nate.

"Members of the community," the Bishop began. "There will not be a wedding taking place between Miriam and Nate, as it appears she has lied about her involvement with him. However, it has come to *mei* attention that Levinia and Nate have something they wish to confess to everyone."

He flashed Levinia a knowing smile.

Levinia looked at Nate. Had he already confessed to the Bishop he'd spent the night with her? They both knew it was innocent, but perhaps he'd neglected to leave that part out to afford the opportunity to marry her.

"Will you marry me?" Nate whispered to her.

"*Jah,* but Miriam took *mei* wedding dress."

"*Ach,* I don't care that you are wearing a maid's uniform. The dress Miriam has on is now tainted and I wouldn't want you to marry me in it. I want to marry you just the way you are."

Happy tears filled Levinia's eyes as he kissed her gently before addressing the community.

"I must confess that I love this woman and would like her to be *mei fraa.*"

He hadn't told of their night together after all.

He *was* an honorable *mann.*

He loved her and wanted to marry her, and not because the community would force it on him. He would marry her because he loved her.

The End

LOOK FOR THE OTHER BOOKS IN THIS SERIES COMING IN 2014

Amish Brides of Willow Creek

Second Chances

Book Two

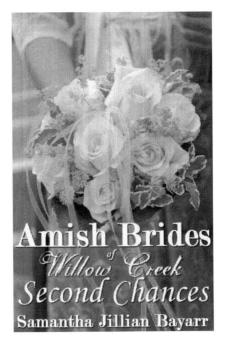

Amish Brides of Willow Creek

Sweet Nothings

Book Three

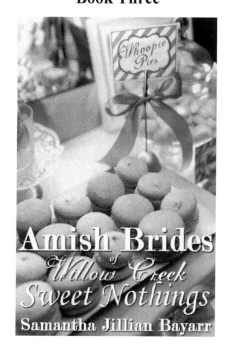

Amish Brides of Willow Creek

Snowflake Bride

Christmas Edition

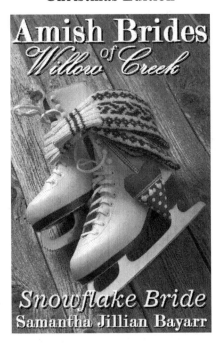

This eBook is now FREE!

This eBook is now FREE!

This eBook is now FREE!

VOLUME ONE

Other Titles by Samantha Bayarr

Jacob's Daughter Amish Series
Jacob's Daughter
Amish Winter Wonderland
Under the Mulberry Tree
Amish Winter of Promises
Chasing Fireflies
Amish Summer of Courage
Under the Harvest Moon

Amish Brides of Willow Creek Series
Amish Brides of Willow Creek: Sibling Rivalry: Book One
Amish Brides of Willow Creek: Second Chances: Book Two
Amish Brides of Willow Creek: Sweet Nothings: Book Three
Amish Brides of Willow Creek: Snowflake Bride: Christmas Edition

Amish Winter Collection
An Amish Christmas Wish
Amish White Christmas
Amish Love Letters

LWF Amish Series
Little Wild Flower: Book One
Little Wild Flower: Book Two
The Taming of a Wild Flower: Book Three
Unto Others: Companion Edition
Little Wild Flower in Bloom
Little Wild Flower's Journey

The Quilter's Son series
The Quilter's Son: Book One: Liam's Choice
The Quilter's Son: Book Two: Lydia's Heart
The Quilter's Son: Book Three: Nathan's Apprentice
The Quilter's Son: Book Four: Maddie's Quilt
The Quilter's Son: Nellie's Legacy
The Quilter's Son: Ethan's Pride

Christian Romance

Milk Maid in Heaven

The Anniversary

A Sheriff's Legacy: Book One (Historical)

Preacher Outlaw: Book Two (Historical)

Made in the USA
Lexington, KY
14 August 2014